AFRICAN ART
OF THE
DOGON

Village of Banani from cliffs at Bongo

Granaries, cliffs and caves at Ireli

AFRICAN ART
OF THE
DOGON

The Myths of the Cliff Dwellers

JEAN LAUDE

9783

Foreword by Lester Wunderman

A Studio Book

The Brooklyn Museum in association
with
The Viking Press
New York

Toguna, men's meeting house

Translation by Joachim Neugroschel. Photographs by Richard di Liberto. Dogon Sculpture from the collection of Lester Wunderman. Organized by Michael Kan, Curator of Primitive Art and New World Cultures, The Brooklyn Museum

Thanks are due to Eliot Elisofon for making available his superb visual material on the Dogon, to Duncan F. Cameron, Director of The Brooklyn Museum, for his support and encouragement, and to all members of the museum staff, who have rendered valuable assistance. Especial thanks go to Sylvia Hochfield, Sylvia Williams, Mary Ann Durgin, Beatrice Brailsford, and Bernard Wolff for their untiring work on this project.

MICHAEL KAN

Preface

The late 1960s and early 1970s have witnessed highly important developments in the study of African art. No longer content to study the individual object apart from its cultural context, we now seek to relate it to a more total experience, often a ritual process involving performing arts such as music, recitation, and dance. These developments are clearly reflected in the new directions taken by museums in the planning of African art exhibitions. We are moving away from the more superficial "masterpiece" show, which emphasizes only fine objects removed from their African context, to exhibitions stressing more specialized, in-depth studies of African art, subdivided according to geography, material, or the larger cultural complexes in which it functions, while still not sacrificing aesthetic quality.

In the 1973 exhibition organized by The Brooklyn Museum, which focused exclusively on the art and culture of the Dogon, the museum continued a tradition of interest in African art that dates back to the earliest African art exhibition in America, in 1922. The Dogon objects in the exhibition, and in this book, were collected by Lester Wunderman in Africa, America, and Europe within the last decade, and to the best of our knowledge constitute the finest and most complete assemblage of Dogon sculpture in private hands. Perhaps even more unusual than his collection is Mr. Wunderman's interest in the Dogon themselves. Few collectors of African art have ever taken the trouble to discover at first hand the creators of the art in their collection, but the superb photographs of the Dogon and their country taken by Mr. Wunderman speak most eloquently of his enduring interest in the Dogon as a living people.

MICHAEL KAN,
Curator of Primitive Art and New World Cultures,
The Brooklyn Museum

Baobab trees, houses and granaries in village of Sanga

Thatched tops of granaries at Songo

Foreword

The great bend of the Niger River in Mali flows between some of the most miraculous places on earth. There sits Mopti, a river marketplace, the "Venice of the Niger," and farther on is Timbuktu, legendary capital of ancient empires and one of the cradles of civilization.

Also there, less than two hundred miles from Timbuktu, and just a few tortuous hours' drive from Mopti, one enters the land, the cliffs, and the life of the Dogon—a people and countryside like no other on earth. It is a journey beyond conventional time and space.

Even at ten miles an hour the road is almost impassable. No wider than a path, its natural surface of sharp angular rock shelves introduces the craggy escarpments and formidable cliffs that lie ahead, and the black and red earth, flooded in the rainy season, and baked in turn by arid months under the sub-Saharan sun, seems ancient and more abused than any land one has seen before.

Bandiagara, the official and most populous village of the Dogon area, is really only the entry point. Here the road is as level as the surrounding savannah, but as one drives on, past the small river at Andiambolo, the landscape suddenly becomes magical. Giant boulders are strewn at ran-

11

dom everywhere, almost as if they had been rolled there in some mad celestial bowling match. The aged trees, tortured in shape by their struggle to survive, blend into the landscape. Wood and stone become indistinguishable from each other in contour and texture.

Great baobab trees, in circumference as large as giant redwoods, grow to a height of only thirty feet. They are bent and set at odd angles as if pressed into the earth upside down and askew by some giant jest of nature. From their gnarled trunks grow leafless branches, which in turn branch again, until the tree tops appear to be intricate root systems planted in the air. They leaf only in the rainy season.

In the distance, the great cliffs rising abruptly vertical to almost a thousand feet, pockmarked with thousands of caves and concealing scores of villages, begin to be visible almost as a mirage in the flame of the sun. Seeing them, you think of the walled towns of Europe and realize that here is not a fortress town, but a fortress country, which the tides of history smashed against but could not essentially alter.

Along the road, amidst the rocks and trees, the Dogon people begin to appear, raising one arm in a gesture of welcome. All at once there are villages, and the earth is a checkerboard of small, green, tilled plots of land. You hear the rhythmic thump of the millet pounders, the high-pitched chatter of children, the bleating of the ever-present Dogon sheep with their white bodies and black heads. The smell of smoke, cooking fires, hot earth, and indigo dyes is everywhere. The landscape is transformed from a setting for a fable to a real world of interaction between the forces of nature and the vitality of man.

For me, this visit to the Dogon country was the culmination of an experience that had begun almost two decades before. From the day I saw and acquired my first piece of Dogon sculpture in a gallery in Los Angeles, to the day I found myself bouncing along this wild, remote dirt track, my path had led to the Dogon.

It was at first an adventure in artistic discovery. Upon acquiring my first piece, I wanted to know more about the people who had carved it and why. Dogon sculpture had striking similarities to Picasso, Modigliani, Giacometti, and the German Expressionists. Was this simply accident or coincidence? How did it manage to be geometric, abstract, and naturalistic all at the same time? If this art was a language, what did it say? Who had said it—and when? Why was Dogon art called primitive or ethnographic? What was primitive—the art, the artist, the society he lived in? (Who decides what is primitive anyway?) Each question raised another, and answers were hard to find.

12

The few books in English then available on African art briefly mentioned the Dogon as great and mysterious artists of the African cliffs. The many French studies of the Dogon were mostly unavailable and untranslated. These derived chiefly from the studies made in the 1920s and 1930s by Marcel Griaule and his colleagues at the Musée de l'Homme and repeated or built on his work without confirming or modifying his findings. Early German texts from around the turn of the twentieth century referred to the Dogon as the *Habe*, showed a few examples of their art, and left it at that.

These were serious difficulties for a beginning collector. I resolved then (as I still believe) that my interest in Dogon art was to grow from my own response to it—however uninformed that response might be. During all these subsequent years, as I have searched museums, libraries, auctions, private collections, and the inventories of large and small art dealers here and abroad, my feelings have never changed. The art of the Dogon had touched me emotionally and aesthetically—and continues to do so to this day.

The collection shown here was never planned to be what it has become. I collected Dogon art whenever I could find pieces that I judged to be aesthetically satisfying, authentic, and representative. The collection finally came to contain many good, several great, and a few totally unique pieces of Dogon art. As a whole, it allows one to see the many subjects and forms of the art of the Dogon people, in all the materials they used.

It is a misfortune that one sees and perceives such art out of context, whether it be in a museum, a gallery, a book, or one's home. Among the Dogon people, in the Dogon landscape, in the context of Dogon belief, these sculptures take on their true relevance and status. A figure with arms reaching toward the heavens has a unique significance in a land without rain or reservoirs, parched for half the year. A figure wrought in iron is not a simple abstraction if the smith who forged it is believed to have descended directly from his remote predecessor who brought the secret of ironmaking down from heaven itself. A couple carved in wood is not a simple portrait, or an exercise in aesthetics, when it represents the twins born of the first perfect union between the god and earth and symbolizes the Dogon belief in the reciprocity of male and female, man and nature, young and old, earth and sky, the living and those who have lived before.

A mask should never be regarded as beautiful or ugly when it is detached from the dancer and the dance. It was not meant to be seen at rest. It is theater, drama, life, spirit, and ritual. To watch Dogon dancers emerging from the cliffs and caves in their brilliant costumes, to hear the rhythm of the drums,

13

and to experience the masks and dancers in motion, is to witness an artistic event equal to any in the world.

Dogon art can hardly be called primitive. It contributes to expanding and enriching the life of those for whom it is carved; it is an integral part of Dogon society. Nor is that society, as I saw it, necessarily primitive either. It may not be technologically oriented, but that is another matter. It is simply another course, an alternative method of human organization. To me, it seemed more loving, more peaceful, and more at ease with its environment, its institutions, and its neighbors than ours. The Dogon conceive heaven as being just like earth.

As John Dewey observed: "The hostility to association of fine art with normal processes of living is a pathetic, even a tragic, commentary on life as it is normally lived. Only because that life is usually so stunted, aborted, slack or heavy laden, is the idea entertained that there is some inherent antagonism between the process of normal living and creation and enjoyment of works of aesthetic art."

Assembling the collection was a process of continuous discovery and learning, in which I was assisted by many friends, scholars, collectors, and dealers who knew of my special interest in the Dogon. To name just a few: Eliot. Elisofon, artist and Africanist, who helped me learn to see; Michael Kan, Curator of Primitive Art and New World Cultures at The Brooklyn Museum, whose professional vision and personal energy and determination brought the first exhibition of this collection into being at the museum. The counsel and encouragement of Dr. Pascal James Imperato and Dr. Hans Guggenheim were invaluable. While the pieces in the collection were discovered and acquired in many places—and from many sources—indispensable and primary assistance came from Henri Kamer, a great art dealer, whose advice, help, judgment, and ability to locate great art have really made this collection possible.

I hope that the opportunity to see one hundred pieces of Dogon art and photographs of the Dogon country and Dogon life will provide others with a small window into the great art and unique life of the Dogon of Mali—these great artists of the African cliffs.

— LESTER WUNDERMAN

14

Ancient houses and round granaries built into the cliffs at Ireli

Funeral at Amani

The Myths of the Cliff Dwellers

". . . the secret adventures of order . . ."
—Jorge Luis Borges

Our age did not invent the "museum without walls"; we merely gave it a name and expanded its content. We are now interested in the arts that Leonardo da Vinci and Dürer misunderstood or ignored, in spite of their curiosity about exotic things. Nevertheless, we see these works from a distance since they were not conceived by the genius of the West. Thus, although we preserve their fundamental originality, we exile them to specialized areas of research or group them into vast aggregates with vague outlines. Where areas are too specialized, certain features, arbitrarily emphasized, have hidden the others and reconstituted an illusory unity. With aggregates that are too broad, the more precise the inquiry, the more elusive the reality of the whole.

This has been the fate of "Negro art." Since the beginning of the century, objects of extremely varying quality and diverse origin have been grouped together according to the same image. Scholars, in trying to avoid the sterile repetition of generalities, have abandoned an overall but superficial view of these objects for more exact studies of limited areas. The intensive method has prevailed; hasty syntheses based on unsorted and unimportant material have given way to specialized monographs.

17

The field of investigation was soon reduced to the art of a single society, then to a single aspect of that art. This reaction, although salutary, has led to other excesses. Most gravely, it has neglected a difficult methodological problem raised by Georges Dumézil when he pointed out that monographs cannot be produced with assurance until an overall order has been recognized. The monograph and the study of the whole must proceed together and continually modify each other.

The study of the sculpture attributed to the Dogon must be approached with the greatest caution. Although we have considerable information about Dogon culture, most of it refers to rites and myths from the region of Sanga alone, and it is all in the form of narratives—narratives related by native informants and then written down by investigators, thus undergoing a double interpretation. We should never forget Rousseau's profound remark in his *Essai sur l'origine des langues*: "What the ancients said most vividly they did not express with words but by signs; they did not tell, they showed."

As material testimonies, the objects mitigate the absence of a written literature and direct research toward problems that have perhaps not received sufficient attention. The country—a geographical concept—does not necessarily coincide with the society, at least not in Black Africa, where cultures are intertwined rather than merged, where animistic beliefs coexist but do not combine in a true syncretism. The Dogon country is occupied by various peoples who regulate their mutual relations—human, political, or even religious—by systems that seem to us complex and are today partially destroyed. Behind an apparent present unity, we can sometimes discern, through the information furnished by an object, certain perspectives that history has introduced or displaced, that society has regulated, organized, and given significance.

Works collected or even carved in the cliff country of the Dogon are not necessarily Dogon in origin or even meant for use there. Stylistic variations—or rather the presence of certain formal determinants—often show that this country, difficult of access, was once the scene of events that have left living traces in the culture of its people. It was not one of the high places where the purity of a doctrine was jealously preserved, but a refuge and not always an effective one. The peoples who live here were driven back against the Bandiagara Cliff, and their contacts with other cultures (African and perhaps Mediterranean) must be taken into account. Their sculpture bears witness to these contacts and the exchanges that followed. But it exists also within a temporal continuity and serves to affirm the permanent values of the group. And its products do not have the frequently ephemeral character of masks, which are carved in soft wood and used only on certain occasions.

Historical Background: Myth and History

We have little certain knowledge of the history of the Dogon country; most often conjecture alternates with hypothesis. The external and internal events retained in the memory of a people who have never used writing as a vehicle of thought have been distorted by the mythic imagination by which they are engrossed. Myth integrates historical elements and subjects them to its own framework; that is to say it compels them to fit into its own system. Thus synthesized to the extreme, gathered together in a highly significant form, they arrive at another level of reality.

Is it possible to trace the history of the Dogon country, or should we give up the attempt since the elements are supplied only by oral traditions that have been contaminated and transformed by mythic thought? By granting little documentary value to oral traditions, we run the risk of an arbitrary reconstruction of history. As H. Moniot has pointed out, one must not judge the oral tradition as a whole but make an internal and external analysis of each tradition; one of them might well be sound no matter how venerable, and despite the poor memory of the informant. If oral traditions are treated thus scientifically, they remain indispensable instruments of analysis.

That Africans have neither crystallized nor stimulated their thought through the intermediary of writing cannot be regarded as an omission or an intellectual deficiency. Because this fact is central to the very structure of these cultures, writing is not felt as a necessity in Black Africa. The esoteric nature of thought is seen as imposing a limitation on the transmission and diffusion of information and knowledge. Thought is embodied in and directly communicated by another means: the creation of sculpture.

As they appear to us in the light of research done by Marcel Griaule and his followers, Dogon sculptures embody highly religious ideals, values, and feelings, and would constitute symbolic and esoteric entities, the progressive understanding of which would delineate a path of initiation. Strongly and deeply imbued with religion, symbolism, and esoterism, the Dogon sculptures are akin in function to the art produced in Pharaonic Egypt. But there is a vital difference: Dogon sculpture is not publicly visible. I would suggest that this characteristic constitutes a relevant standard for comparison, related as it is to the absence in the Dogon country of a monumental architecture in stone, that is to say an imperishable architecture.

Esoteric as it was, Pharaonic art was nevertheless manifested in monumental structures that were meant to bear witness to the authenticity and eternal reality of

19

the ideas they embodied. These structures synthesize a conception of the universe of which they offer visible and sufficient images in the form of "reduced models." The same is true for the art of the Dogon, as well as for the Senufo, for whom a series of sculptures serves at the time of initiation to support an explanation of the world and make concrete not only the idea but also the reality of the universe.

"Reduced" as Egyptian models may be in relation to the universe, they are monumental, stable, and immovable. The African works, on the other hand, are much smaller and easily handled, which permits combinations and interpretations of the elements they contain. But while Egyptian works are integrated directly into the landscape and impose their significance on the natural order in a spectacular way, African ones, which have similar synthesizing and signifying functions, are integrated not with nature but with cultures, of which one of the essential characteristics is the invisibility of its system of relationships (interpersonal, intertribal) and of its concept of the human being.

In the Dogon country, the invisible character of the culture is shown by the fact that these pieces are at present hidden from view—concealed in the shadow of sanctuaries, inside family houses, or in the residence of the *hogon* or priest, and exhibited only on rare occasions (although there is evidence that this was not always the case).[1] The transmission of information and knowledge which they make concrete takes place by way of initiation. But here we must take care not to be ensnared by meanings suggested by our own use of words. The initiation does not consist in dispelling one by one the delusions that constitute obstacles to the candidate's knowledge of the ultimate truth, which will then be unveiled to him in a single stroke. It is a formative, pedagogical process such as Plotinus described when he wrote in the *Enneads* that in the mysteries nothing is *revealed* to the initiate, because nothing and no one can make him see what he is fortunate enough to see for himself. But if the priest is wise and understands the enigma, once he has penetrated the sanctuary, he can authenticate the vision that he contemplates there. Initiation for Plotinus is a visual process; hardly anything is spoken. Everything comes to pass as if the candidate were being shown various objects (or participating in various activities or spectacles) and as if his initiation were contingent on the understanding he might thereby derive. Or, as Plotinus explains it, each sign is itself wisdom and reality apprehended at once, not through reasoning or reflection.

1. Louis Desplagnes noted in 1907 that numerous sculptures were visible to the eyes of profane strangers in the dwelling of the *hogon*. "The *hogon* generally lives alone, in a small, highly decorated house which is maintained at the expense of the village and located somewhat apart, often at the summit of a rocky slope. This small monument, the house of the grand priest, adorned with sculptures and reliefs, serves also as a temple to the divinity. . . ." (Desplagnes, 1907, p. 322).

We can on this basis introduce a criticism of the symbolist interpretation of Dogon art, which will permit us to approach more closely to the function of its forms and images. A Dogon does not apprehend form in isolation or as an abstraction. Nor does form illustrate meanings outside of itself; rather, it produces meanings. Just as there is no prerational experience or knowledge of color, there is no prerational knowledge or experience of form. All forms are inscribed in a system that derives from a specific language—the language of art—but this particular language corresponds to a total language that constitutes society itself as a total fact. In Saussure's terms, language is a system of signs that have no material connection with that which they signify. The relationship between the signified and the signifying is conventional, not arbitrary. As Lévi-Strauss has reminded us, "if all art is language, it is not language on the level of conscious thought. All the means at the disposal of the artist constitute so many signs, and the function of the work of art is to signify, to establish a signifying relationship with the object." No art form, whether carved, painted, worked in metal, or danced, refers to a body of ideas or objects existing outside itself. But it can *produce* meanings that can be interpreted in terms of systems regulating cultures foreign to the one in which it was conceived. A celebrated example is supplied by the stone statuettes that the Kissi farmers of Guinea unearth while plowing their fields, and which they adapt to their own cults and interpret as manifestations of their ancestors.

Scientific thoroughness demands the analysis of concrete facts; the interpretations the Dogon offer for these facts are of some interest since they grant us access to the workings of the imagination in a specific culture, but they cannot replace reality. We must recall Lévi-Strauss's warning not to "reduce social reality to the idea that man, even savage man, has of it." If the facts, which for us are the carved objects, are representative, and if our analyses are correct, both will bring us closer to historical problems.

Historical Background: Facts

As Pierre Francastel has pointed out, we generally commit a twofold error when we undertake sociological studies of art. First of all, we pretend to know the real structures of a society, which cannot, in fact, be known without art. Second, we consider art to be an ornament, an accessory, a social superstructure, instead of analyzing it as a fundamental function. These observations might be applied to Dogon art, the product of a society whose real structures are still more alien to us (despite Denise Paulme's fine work) than any society of the Renaissance in the

21

Old village
of Songo

West. We may question the legitimacy of applying them to the study of an art that is undated, in no chronological order, and anonymous, but an examination of the facts serves to answer this objection.

Although we cannot trace a plausible historical framework for the Dogon country, we do have certain general guidelines. The Dogon realize that they are not the first inhabitants of the country they now occupy. Their myths, legends, and traditions retain the memory of their predecessors. The leading part is assigned to small red men whom the Dogon call the Andoumboulu, probably the ancestors of present-day Pygmies. The Andoumboulu were driven out of certain areas by men of normal size, the Tellem, probably the ancestors of the Kurumba of northern Yatenga province. When the Tellem in turn were driven from the Cliff by the Dogon, they left behind, in sanctuaries located on the rocky and almost inaccessible heights, cult and funerary objects that included statuettes. In some places, as soon as weapons were put aside, alliances were established between the invaders and the older inhabitants, and marriages tightened the bonds. In some villages the two populations coexisted peacefully.

The Dogon claim their descent from four families who supposedly populated their present area after fleeing their native region. In the course of their migrations, these families were allegedly attacked by the Mossi and fled northward. Robert Arnaud has dated this migration in the reign of the celebrated Kankan Moussa (1307–32), ruler of the ancient Mali Empire. Denise Paulme confirms this date with a statement made to her in 1935 by an old man in Bandiagara. As reported by the Mossi, the facts are almost identical but causes and circumstances differ.

We can fix a chronological epoch for the migrations and settlement of the Dogon. The formation and expansion of the empire of Mogho-Naba can be dated to the twelfth century. The expansion of Sanga probably occurred in the middle of the twelfth century. Marcel Griaule was able to place the founding of the village of Ibi in the early fifteenth century, perhaps even as early as the beginning of the thirteenth. Furthermore, radiocarbon dating techniques have indicated that certain sculptures discovered in the grottoes of the Cliff and attributed to the Tellem can be placed in the thirteenth century.

It is worthy of note that the chronological epoch to which the oral tradition refers coincides with a known period of upheaval within this region of West Africa. After the death of Kankan Moussa, the Mali Empire, which had flourished during his reign, waned considerably. In 1333 the Mossi of Yatenga pillaged Timbuktu, and the disorder increased until 1336, when Suleiman restored peace. But

24

after his death in 1359 fratricidal struggles lacerated Mali, which, in the fifteenth century, was attacked by the Mossi, the Tuareg, and the Songhai. The Mossi of Yatenga ravaged the eastern provinces; Timbuktu, Arsouane, and Oualata were occupied by the Tuareg in 1443; and in 1465 the Songhai conquered the provinces of the Niger Valley. In 1542 and again in 1546 the Songhai pillaged the province of Bendugu. By 1670 the Mali Empire had vanished from Sudanese history.

Toward the end of the fourteenth century, the West African copper trade with the Maghreb was greatly expanded. This trade had decisive economic and political consequences since the price of copper in Black Africa was now higher than that of gold and more or less the same as that of salt. The demand was so great that when the copper mines in Kano and Takedda were occupied by the Arabs in the fifteenth century, the African nations had to ask the West to supply them with metal in exchange for slaves. Throughout the area of the Niger Bend, copper was the metal needed for mythical and ritual objects.

On the basis of this incomplete information, it is possible to affirm that the Dogon were in contact with other cultures both before their migrations and after they were settled in the Cliff. They were never sheltered and could not isolate themselves. In addition to the Mossi, with whom they often quarreled, and the Tellem, with whom they concluded alliances after defeating them in battle, the Songhai, the Bambara, and the Peuls intervened forcefully in their history. As did Islam; it was in Bandiagara that El-Hadj Omar took refuge after the failure of his holy war, and he died there in 1864. These upheavals, these military and peaceful contacts, obviously had their effect on the myths and the art produced in the Dogon cliff country. If the present state of our knowledge makes it almost impossible to attribute specific mythic features to outside influences, the sculpture obviously retains the traces of foreign impact.

Style and the Metaphysical Foundation

To reconstruct a history of Dogon art is difficult but not impossible, and it is necessary if we wish to reconstruct the history of the people. But first we must return to the problem of symbolism, as it exists not only for the inhabitants of the Dogon country but for a number of peoples claiming the same origin.

Inquiries into the myths, meanings, and functions of a culture have hitherto been undertaken independently of the objects that report mythical events, serve

25

as vehicles for meanings, and assume functions; the objects are then explained as if they were material translations of ideas that might have been translated into another medium. But sculpture produces ideas at the same time that it assures the continuing topicality and permanent reality of mythical events. Although it serves as a material support whenever ideas and events must be commemorated, its role is not limited to that of an archive; it actually reveals what cannot be translated, except, approximately, into terms different from its own. Whatever interpretation may be given by their users, whatever functions may be attributed to them, sculptured objects are specific—and they must be studied as such, in terms of their own language. One must avoid confusing aesthetic theory (such as an art-for-art's-sake approach) with a scientific concept, such as the specificity of artistic objects. As Tynianov noted, the study of art must be the study of the "characteristic features distinguishing art from other provinces of intellectual activity, which function merely as material or as a tool for that study. Every art object represents a complex interaction of numerous factors, and our aim is to define the specific character of that interaction."

All the formal and stylistic, as well as iconographical, variations that occur within the same thematic series are instantly endowed with meaning. Just as there is no one *true* version of a myth, since numerous versions exist which together constitute the myth, so there is no canonical model from which certain sculptures more or less deviate. It would be a grave error to characterize prematurely any Dogon style as "classic," or to treat all the artistic manifestations of the Dogon country in terms of such an abstractly constructed model.

The Cliff people (and traditional Africans in general) think directly with forms, at the very least with signs, more than with words. Consequently, our notion of the relationship between sculptured works and oral myth must be reversed: oral myth arises from sculptured works. I have cited the example of the Senufo. As a more extreme example, among the Chokwe of Angola the initiation rite consists of the presentation to the initiate of a basketful of various objects, including statuettes; nothing is spoken. We might say that the relationship between the object and the myth is a dialectical one: themes connected to the same mythic context interact with the proliferations of meaning attached to specific forms and combinations of forms. Each sculptor combines elements of form in new ways and thus endows the myth with new depth; he discovers new aspects of its inexhaustible profundity.

According to the work of Dominique Zahan, Solange de Ganay, and Germaine Dieterlen, forty-four groups which claim to descend from Mande and which inhabit the territories between the Atlantic Coast, Senegal, and the Niger up to

Dahomey exist on the same "metaphysical foundation." [2] Certain granary shutters (no. 74) have regular rows of forty-four carved figurines on their surface, and it is possible that they can be related to this belief. The shutters are made of two unequal parts (four rows of five figurines on the left, four rows of six figurines on the right) joined together by four strong iron clasps. This arrangement is supposedly an allusion to twinship and to the Primordial Couple (the two parts of the shutter) as well as to the unity of the altar or *binu* in which all who claim to descend from Mande participate. Thus interpreted, the work allegedly constitutes a reminder of the unity of the forty-four peoples and at the same time testifies to their diversity.

If we consult the list of these populations, which include castes (e.g., blacksmiths, weavers, shoemakers), we see that not all of them practice the art of sculpture, and that sculpture, when it exists, varies from one culture to another. Iconographic richness is distributed unevenly among the peoples descended from Mande. Some themes are common to the art of the Dogon, the Senufo, and the Bambara, but neither of the latter groups employs certain Dogon themes of great variety and complexity.

We must observe the greatest circumspection in the characterization of styles. It is the object—and the object alone, as a system of forms—which must be analyzed and classified. Even if the village in which the piece was acquired is known, nothing indicates that it was made there or used there. Even if we are certain of the last two points, we must still ask who commissioned it and who used it. Nothing indicates that the person who ordered a particular piece was a Dogon even though a Dogon may be using it. In fact, non-Dogons often commission a Dogon blacksmith for objects which they need for their own cults and on which they impose their own stamp. Jacqueline Delange is probably correct in her assumption that this was the case with certain objects allegedly made for the Peuls. And we know that in other cultures (particularly in the Congo) invaders superimposed their own cults and the related sculptural material on the cults of the people they subjugated.

2. The geographical location of Mande is still an unsolved problem. The Dogon of the Bandiagara Cliff claim that Mande was in the west, in the area of Bamako; those of the Hombori region place it in the east. Other peoples of the Niger Bend, such as the Kurumba of Yoro and of the Kano region (Aribinda) also claim descent from Mande; the former assert it was in the west and the latter locate it in the east, beween Say and Niamey. According to C. Monteil, the term "Mande" did not refer to a country or a political entity but meant "the residence of the king." This would imply that the word and its variants referred to various locations serving or having served in the past as royal residences or chief towns. According to Dominique Zahan, "Mande plays the role of a creator deity and the people descended from this country are, like the Creation, dispersed over the earth."

The Problem of Attribution

At the outset we are confronted with a twofold problem: the identity of the sculptors to whom we owe that part of the material which is attributed to the Tellem, and the possible influence of this presumably Tellem art on the art of the Dogon newcomers. Another problem is the extreme stylistic and formal diversity of the sculpture attributed to the Dogon, a diversity that can nevertheless be encompassed in an overall unity.

There is positive data to support the attribution of certain statuettes with a characteristic cast of features to the Tellem. When questioned, the Dogon decline to give an opinion about the authorship of these works, which they attribute to their predecessors. We may wonder if these sculptures represent a formative stage of their own artistic development. Such a supposition implies an evolution of Dogon art in the twelfth century, the earliest time to which documents give us access. In very rare cases, we know exactly where the statuettes were discovered. Pierre Langlois, who brought out the first "Tellem" statuettes to appear on the market, always indicated the exact location of his discoveries. Caves had been hollowed out in the cliffs. Rockslides had made them difficult to enter, sometimes inaccessible. It was in these grottoes that he discovered the statuettes, bound into bundles with iron chains, well protected from weather, humidity, and insects under the rock shelter, and preserved also by their thick coat of sacrificial patina (the dried libation of blood and millet gruel). The antiquity of these works is plausible and probable. The Dogon regard these caves as sacred places and never venture into them, even when they are accessible. These tombs and sanctuaries do not belong to them.[3]

These facts allow us to assign a fairly certain Tellem origin to a particular group of sculptures. To the information supplied by outside observation, we can add the sparse data gleaned from morphological and thematic analysis. These presumably Tellem statuettes form a group with certain characteristic stylistic features, relatively clearly defined. They show a preference for certain themes and appear to be iconographically homogeneous. But these elements are insufficient to provide real criteria.

3. According to Dogon myth, it was the Andoumboulu who taught the Tellem metallurgy as well as the art of building homes in hollowed-out cliffs and using iron chains or long, fine ropes to haul things up and down the precipices. The Tellem were supposedly of the same branch as the Kurumba, who were well-known blacksmiths. Among the blacksmiths of the Bandiagara Cliff, we can distinguish two types: those who live together in groups either in a separate part of the village or in villages of their own, and isolated individual craftsmen. Only the former melt iron; the latter merely work it.

Horsemen on the Bandiagara road

Such is the core of the problem. Unable to analyze a sufficient number of works produced within the same population, scholars have characterized the art of a given culture by the dominant features of the little material they knew. For a long time the sculpture of the Dogon country was characterized on the basis of examples published by Carl Kjersmeier in 1935. In 1954, however, new material appeared, and the image that had been formed of the art of the Dogon country was modified. We know now that works once regarded as typical are not necessarily the most representative nor do they constitute the dominant style. On the other hand, they can be understood only in terms of the context and function of other sculptures from which they differ in type.

The statuary of the Dogon country is very diverse. Upon analysis, however, a unity seems to emerge which encompasses the most varied formulas. Is this unity real? Is it characteristic of a culture with clearly defined features in which variants and deviations are successfully integrated? Art and culture are intimately linked. Art is not a social superstructure which reflects the spiritual state of a culture; it is a formative element of culture and one of its fundamental functions. We cannot begin with a conception of the culture of the Dogon country and then discover how artistic productions are more or less harmoniously integrated. We must investigate how artistic creations, as products of an activity and a function, affect the environment they transform and help to create.

The connection between the diversity of formulas and unity of style needs analysis. The style, the entire set of formal criteria that permits us to identify a sculpture of the Dogon country, is the result of diverse trends or formulas. It is not a constraining standard to which all expression must yield.

It is time now to turn our attention to the *producer*. I use this term rather than *artist* or *creator*, which would imply a premature value judgment and involve an ideology. Griaule made some observations, but did not, it seems to me, draw all the necessary conclusions. It is mainly through the work of William Fagg and Michel Leiris that we can approach the problem on a new basis.

First of all, the margin for innovation available to the Black African sculptor is greater than had generally been assumed. At least theoretically, each producer can be distinguished from the others. The anonymity of what was once called "Negro art" is merely a convenient prejudice that masks our ignorance and obstructs a concrete approach. Undoubtedly, the Black African producer has never enjoyed the exorbitant status that the West has conferred on its artists since the Renaissance. But the relative individualization of artistic production must not be underestimated; it has its own value and its effects are far from negligible.

30

Leiris distinguished two categories of producer: professionals, such as black-smiths, who in many groups also do fine work in wood, and official overseers, who often make magico-religious objects (as among the Baluba of the Congo). Masks, on the other hand, are often the work of nonspecialists, young men called upon to make them at the time of their initiation under the guidance of their elders. In the Dogon country, it is a specialist, the blacksmith, who makes statuettes—and only statuettes; he is not qualified to carve masks. But he is not a magician; he does not work in secret under the protection of mysterious powers. As Griaule points out, he is an artisan, indeed an artist, and each man's taste satisfies a particular clientele. There is no question of a secret art secure from imagination, fashion, or other influences.

There are many producers, and each is unique. Thus the problem of formal diversity shifts to the users or clients, who choose among the specialists the one with whom they will place an order. The choice is based on taste and carried out with the help of aesthetic judgment. Even when it is influenced by financial considerations, as when a poor man must content himself with a modest object, it still contains an idea of aesthetic value. The degree of success or complexity of the object is influenced by the wealth of the client.

The problem of the heterogeneity of formulas can be clearly stated on these foundations, as can the problems of the attribution to the Tellem of sculptures with a characteristic cast of features. The objects discovered in the supposedly Tellem sanctuaries can be grouped in relatively distinct series. We can assume the existence of studios where models that constituted a style were elaborated. But the presumed Tellem sculptures are confined to themes of lesser variety than the Dogon sculptures, and all of the Tellem themes recur in Dogon statuary, handled in terms of different formulas.

The term "theme" refers to the iconic appearance of the work and should not be identified with the true meaning of the work attributed to it by the Dogon. An identical theme, e.g., a mother and child, illustrated by sculptures produced in different cultures does not necessarily have the same significance or value in all cases. Even within the same culture, the function and the meaning of a specific theme can vary according to historical and social fluctuations. Nothing permits us to affirm—or even to imagine—that the meaning now given to statuettes with raised arms is identical to the meaning originally given them by the Tellem. The sculpture produces meanings. When a new theme occurs, either through innovation or borrowing, it does not disrupt the system it enters; it becomes an integral part of it. When it is borrowed, its original meaning is distorted or even totally

31

denied, and it is reconverted into the mythic system that receives it. Iconographical analyses are thus of little use, especially when the same themes are present in different cultures, and it is all the more difficult when we have no historical framework in which to situate the levels of meaning that envelop a particular theme.

Nor have we any criteria furnished by an analysis of forms that would enable us to arrange variations of meaning and function chronologically; we cannot place these forms in a logical and continuous line of succession. For lack of sufficient guidelines that would permit critical discussion, we must renounce any evolutional or genetic hypothesis. To make formulas follow one another as though they were the result of an internal and necessary development would be to contaminate the facts with the hypothesis they were supposed to confirm. We cannot, *a priori*, regard the existence of styles as organic and autonomous. The heterogeneity of formulas may actually be devoid of chronological significance; it may just as easily result from the multiplicity and disparity of studios and local traditions.

The variety of formulas used to treat a single theme shows the existence of a choice and a quest. The same models are not indefinitely repeated. Formal variations observable within a thematic series are often considerable and are by no means limited to minor details; they frequently involve the basic structure itself.

II

The Dogon material with which we are familiar can be classified on the basis of technical, formal, thematic, and stylistic criteria. First of all, we can group the works according to the material from which they have been produced. It seems to me that a link exists between the tools and technique of the producer and the stylistic tendencies of the work. One must not carry too far Gottfried Semper's view that material, technique, and utilitarian purpose define style. Alois Riegl was reacting to this mechanistic theory when he characterized style as *will* that expresses itself through such limiting factors. He placed the emphasis on the creative aspect and the choice of formal systems. Different peoples making sculpture with the same purpose, with identical materials and similar techniques, produce works that are stylistically diverse. Different formal systems should be seen as the result not of greater or lesser technical, intellectual, or aesthetic capacity but of diversely directed will. But it is no less true, as Henri Focillon has written, that "raw materials carry their own destiny or a certain formal vocation." Pro-

32

The Primordial Couple seated on an
imago mundi stool (cat. no. 37).

Dancers at the village of Bongo

Funeral dance at Kamba-Bandié featuring stilt
dancer and dancers wearing Kanaga masks

Rock paintings from the walls of the Circumcision Grotto above the village of Songo

vided that the artist is not deliberately working against that "formal vocation," he will not achieve the same results when carving as when modeling or working with iron.

Modeling

William Fagg has divided the arts of Black Africa into three major groups: Sudanese, Guinean, and Congolese. The arts of the Dogon country belong to the Sudanese group. They are distinguished by a relative lack of nonferrous metals and the use of simple tools. In cultures in which modeling is the major mode of production, in the form of terracotta or lost-wax (*cire perdue*) casting, techniques derive from the additive method. The producer starts with the inner core and by gradually adding to it brings the form to its completion. These cultures flourished primarily in regions where there was access to copper, gold, and tin mines, an area stretching from Guinea to Nigeria.

In the Dogon country, figurative pieces modeled in clay are, so far as we know, extremely rare. Aside from the example in the de Ménil Collection (Laude, 1971, p. 51, fig. 35), the very fine head shown here (no. 68) is unique. It is thought to have been unearthed on the border between Wahigouya and the Dogon country, near the village of Kani Kombolé, where, according to tradition, the four families, the Arou, Ono, Dyon, and Domno, rested after their migration. Kani Kambolé is near Kani Bonzon and the now destroyed village of Kani Na, where the first altar to the serpent Lébé was set up and shared by the four families. Two other terracotta figures were found in Djenné and Mopti; one is now in the I.F.A.N. Museum in Dakar and the other in the Rasmussen Collection, Paris (Laude, 1971, p. 50, figs. 33, 34). According to Raymond Mauny, they may be dated to the twelfth century. Mounds in the same region have recently been rifled by pot-hunters and have yielded beautiful terracottas, which have been dispersed before we could learn their place of origin or archaeological context.

These objects present a problem because they are still too few in number to be analyzed or characterized stylistically, and their early date precedes the arrival of the Dogon to the Cliff. Furthermore, all available facts lead us to conclude that there must have been a long tradition of terracotta, from the Niger Basin to Chad, where it lasted until about the fifteenth century (among the Sao of Chad). A change in technology may have accompanied social change; terracotta became woman's work, and the potter is now as a rule the blacksmith's wife. It is possible that the arrival from elsewhere of artisans in iron, technologically better equipped,

37

had an effect on West African societies. This may have something to do with the existence in the Dogon country of two separate classes of blacksmiths. We know that in Meroë, Nubia, the slag heaps were located near the Temple of the Sun and that the priests were ironworkers. We know also that in the twelfth century East Africa stopped supplying India with iron, a commerce that had existed since the eighth century. Could a migration of iron-working peoples have taken place in the twelfth century, presumably for economic reasons? If so, it would have diffused not only more complex techniques but also fragments of mythology, which would have inspired the imagination of the peoples among whom the new-comers settled and where they enjoyed a special status. This would explain the link that was set up and institutionalized between the female potter and the blacksmith, the two specialists particularly charged with producing religious and cult objects. A noteworthy fact of West African life is that the new does not supersede the old but is superimposed upon it and even joined to it. The most striking example is the quasi-priestly institution of the "masters of the soil," individuals who are appointed to mediate between the present users of the soil and its most ancient inhabitants, the original people to whom its care was granted in the beginning.

For the moment, all this is pure conjecture. But, as far as we can judge from the tiny number of terracottas found in the Djenné-Mopti-Bandiagara triangle, there seems to be a stylistic break between these works and the wood carvings. The rupture strikes me as the result of both a change in tradition and a switch to a different technique. Wood is a substance that resists facility of execution, and prevents the sculptor from making a faithful reproduction, which—concealed as it will be in the dwelling—is not an aim of the Dogon, but leads to the production of *plastic equivalents*. The naturalistic tendency that flourished, for example, in the art of Ife was encouraged by the ductility and supple sensuality of a material that neither resisted nor opposed the artist's hand. More so than the carver, the modeler appears to be conducting a dialogue with the material he is about to animate; his hands linger on the surfaces to which they transmit their inflections without need of an intermediary. Clay and wax are passive; the modeler com-municates directly with the surface of his work, yet it is a long, dreaming soliloquy that imposes its profound message on the being it will embody.

The *cire perdue* method proceeds from modeling. A number of the copper and brass objects included here, mainly rings and bracelets but also a few figures, raise certain questions. If we limit ourselves to iconography, certain of them reveal Dogon themes: a horseman on a ring (no. 78), a squatting figure holding his head in his hands (no. 2). But the horseman turns up also in the art of the Bambara, the Senufo, and the Songhai. In Songhai myth, the horseman and his mount both have the head of a vulture; a ring similar to the one shown here was acquired in 1948 in Songhai country by Jean Rouch and is now in the Musée de l'Homme, Paris. The Dogon and the Songhai are linked by institutional bonds that encourage exchanges, and these small objects travel easily, so they may well have circulated from one group to another. Even if they do refer back to certain myths, nothing authorizes us to regard them as specifically religious or even cult objects. I realize that copper is used by the Dogon for specific iconographic representations, but the same is true of the Bambara, the Songhai, and the Mossi. At the most, these rings may have been the insignia of dignitaries, or simply tokens of gratitude. The fact that certain of their themes appear also in Dogon sculpture, for example the figure of Dyougou Serou hiding his face after his original act of incest, does not authorize us to maintain that they show Dogon workmanship. These rings and bracelets, produced by the *cire perdue* process, may have originated among the Mossi; the question remains open.

Ironwork

Whereas pieces modeled in clay or cast in copper by the *cire perdue* process exhibit a definite taste for supple and rounded surfaces, those in forged iron reveal completely different formal conceptions. There are far too few of them to permit even the sketchiest of classifications. Those shown here, with one exception (no. 9), are made of a single piece of iron; no element was welded or riveted. We do not yet know how the metal was purified, but we must emphasize the virtuosity of the ironworker, his skill in using very simple tools (such as tongs and hammer) to bend the rigid metal into supple rods with unexpected, taut curves, his ability to make the bars yield to his design by removing from the incandescent mass the elements that stand out like the branches of a tree.

These elongated figures that threaten to dissolve in space at any moment nevertheless stretch upward like seeds of growth and bear witness to an unerring plastic inventiveness. As soon as the suggestions and possibilities of the material have been developed, they yield to the guiding will, which explores the semantic possibilities in the constellation of themes, extending the range of knowledge. These works are devoid of expressionism except in an abstract sense; they were conceived not in fear and trembling but to authenticate the life of the individual and of the group and to give it meaning, that is direction and significance, by integrating it into the continuous chain of mythic events, a chain that asserts the reality of myth. Only the line is expressive, in Matisse's sense of the word: alive, sensitive, but controlled and intellectual.

The artist is always careful to respect the fundamental structures imposed on him by his themes, their meanings and values. These fundamental structures are part of him; they are components of his creative being. But even when the works approach so closely to these structures as to display them almost naked in their purity (a Westerner would say abstract or conceptual), they are never reduced to schema, to diagrams.

The same artists who made these slender, flexible signs in iron and who also work in wood fashion the objects in broad architectural rhythms, in spite of their small size, by employing rich, contrasting volumes, which seem to be nourished from inside and at the same time stretched just below their surfaces and across their visible contours. The multiplicity and diversity of techniques and solutions testify to a creative and aesthetic sensibility that is highly sophisticated, even though the works were not intended for mere enjoyment.

The few iron pieces now coming to light may signal the beginning of a profound upheaval in our present knowledge. It is too soon to appreciate the full scope of the phenomenon, but we can say that the very high aesthetic quality of the works cannot be fortuitous or sporadic. The technical mastery of the artists who created these pieces is accompanied by undeniable inventiveness and aesthetic awareness. Even when they served ritual or cult purposes, with their themes dictated by their function, these works eloquently reveal that they were made by true artists. They would not have been possible or even conceivable if an extremely sure taste had not already been developed, if plastic experiments had not been perfected and their results transmitted and accepted.

These works were generally affixed above the façade of totemic altars or sanctuaries (*binu*), but they also form integral parts of certain statuettes to which they were attached (e.g. Langlois, 1954, p. 58, fig. 46). There is some indication that they were once used as weapons in ritual sacrifices. Their function was similar perhaps to the function attributed to the *edan* emblems of the Ogboni Society of the Nigerian Yoruba, which are related to beliefs concerning twinship. Those that depict animals and are not extended on a long rod were most likely set up on family altars next to cult vessels (nos. 82, 83). Iconographically, they are extremely varied. Some have tusks, most frequently double, each branch ending in a narrow coil: the image of the horned forehead of the heavenly ram (no. 20). Others have a rod elongated by a piece of flat iron and branches, curving inward, which enclose a figure with raised arms and sawtooth-fingered hands (no. 9).

This piece recalls both the anvil and the blacksmith's scrap iron. The arms relate it to the image of the water spirit; they probably played the same role as the coiled ends of the tusks. Other specimens are more complex, more directly figurative, and relate iconographically to wooden statuary.

Carving

Wood carving is what William Fagg calls a "subtractive method." As Focillon describes it, the producer, working from the outside, seeks the form inside the block. The block exists before the sculpture, and the dimensions of the sculpture cannot exceed those of the block from which it is hewn. Although Dogon sculptors produced statuettes only from single pieces of timber, their dimensions are often relatively large. The posts of the men's house (*toguna*) may be six feet in height (nos. 70–72). Thus the small size of the statuettes is the result of choice, not technical limitation.

Although it is not felt as a limitation on the size of the work, the tree trunk from which the sculpture is hewn does propose a form. Before becoming an ancestor or a demiurge riding his cosmic steed or the Primordial Couple, a Dogon sculpture is a piece of wood occupying a specific location in space. Perhaps the tree trunk is acknowledged and its bend or curve survives; sometimes even the knots and the forks of branches are integrated into the sculpture. Or else the limits of the volume continue to exist only abstractly in the mind and do not coincide with the surfaces of the carved object. But even though the original block is three-dimensional, the sculptor does not necessarily conceive his statuette by giving it depth; a single surface can sometimes accommodate all the required signs.

Statistically, Dogon art is essentially an art of wood sculpture. I know of only two sculptures carved in stone. One of them, in the Tishman Collection (Laude, 1964, p. 48, fig. 1), was acquired in Sanga but was probably used in another village in the Dogon country. The other is shown here (no. 29). Their high degree of skill and workmanship prove that these pieces are not isolated attempts without precedents. The Tishman piece is dominated by an unusual head that does not exhibit the characteristic traits of Dogon sculpture as we know it. The piece shown here is a stone carved in relief on all four sides; on each of the long sides are two figures with arms at their sides, and on each short side is a single figure. The whole composition refers to the four pairs of *nommos* and the Primordial Couple. The six figures all have distinctively Tellem features.

The similarity may be accidental, but the fact remains that these stone works evoke certain objects, also carved and of the same character, discovered in the Kissi country of Guinea. The Kissi, according to the Dogon, are also descendants of Mande. Dieterlen claims that stone sculptures were buried in the ground to mark the allegiance of the countries where they have been found to the ancient Mali Empire, but they have been unearthed in quantity only in the Kissi country and the Mende country. Too few have been found elsewhere for us to accept the idea as more than hypothesis.

The Blacksmith

The more deeply we investigate the arts of Black Africa, especially those of the Dogon country, the more clearly we discern the features of an individual, all the more enigmatic because he is apparently so familiar, who seems to hold in his grasp some of the keys to the culture while remaining mute—or almost mute—about them. The blacksmith, for that is who he is, soon appears as a central figure, placed squarely at the crux of some of the major problems posed by Black African civilizations. We cannot reduce his role to that of a simple craft without seriously distorting it; yet this role, in its rich, complex implications, must be grasped in its material reality, in the historical context that its appearance seems to have modified, as well as in the rich flowering of mythic depictions that bind his technical function to a network of relationships between the visible and invisible worlds, the living and the dead, and between human beings themselves.

Among all the peoples descended from Mande, the blacksmith is more than merely a technician to whom the farmer (like the warrior before him) turns for his tools and weapons. He occupies a special place, like a demiurge or a civilizing hero, in the various myths of origin. He assumes social responsibilities that make him a true intercessor, a mediator (among the Bambara it is normally a blacksmith who heads the Kono initiation society). He is the man who cares for equipment and who alone is able to manufacture it. The agricultural life and military security of the country are dependent on him, as is ritual activity, for he is the specialist from whom one commissions statuettes, religious and ritual paraphernalia, and objects used during initiation ceremonies. Thus he is also a sculptor, because he has at his disposal the necessary technical equipment and because, in the mythic and ritual order, he is, as I have said, the intercessor, the mediator.

These few notes may help to elucidate some of the problems posed by the formal and stylistic diversity of Dogon art. Certain works, if they are to be carved, require more varied and complex tools. The presumed Tellem works are conceived as a single volume with a plain back; they require simpler tools than the monumental figures. Compare no. 25, for example, with the magnificent couple shown as no. 37.

We would be repeating the errors of nineteenth-century evolutionism if we denied aesthetic quality to works fashioned with rudimentary tools. Nor can we assume these works are older simply because the tools used to make them were more elementary. All we can say is that these works perpetuate the memory of more archaic traditions. This, however, says a great deal; we are envisaging the existence of a chronological frontier, fluid and uncertain, separating two stages of culture. We are allowing ourselves, therefore, at least by way of a hypothesis, to situate in time and space a material that has come down to us without definite records. Everything leads us to believe that at some point the technology of the peoples now inhabiting the Dogon country improved perceptibly, either because new mines were discovered or new methods were perfected for extracting and smelting the metal, or because newly arrived technicians revolutionized the practice of metallurgy.

To some extent, tools affect the aesthetic pattern of the art object; the carving technique imposes its own implications, restraining (or broadening) the possibilities open to the sculptor. In the carving technique, we can observe a process parallel to the method that in Dogon thought regulates the passage from the general to the particular. The sculptor gradually releases an anthropomorphic image which becomes more and more particularized by means of conventional signs that, taken as a whole, constitute a repertoire (or a code), and convey a message. On the ideological level, this combination of signs is related to a system of classifications; on the technical level it depends, however, on the possibilities of the tools employed. Dogon sculpture, ruled by this idea of assemblage or "montage," could only have been fashioned with tools adapted for the purpose, which did not necessarily impart this idea. The tools used do not necessarily impose this notion; rather, their use permitted only the realization in sculpture of a tendency otherwise inherent in modes of thought and belief.

To sum up, the various techniques with which the Dogon sculptor works are components of style but do not determine it. Other elements are involved, not so much on the metaphysical or cosmogonic level as on that of the functioning of symbols within formal systems. It is on this underlying level that we can grasp the real structures of the sculpture of the Dogon country. An important problem that requires study, one that would permit a more complex approach to the sculpture, is the question of the proportions of the works. Everything seems to indicate that these proportions are not due to chance and are by no means arbitrary, but neither are they deliberate or determined in advance. They reveal themselves to be organizing elements of perception and signs of a particular conception of the world and of the role conferred on carved objects, which appear to be, as Lévi-Strauss puts it, genuine "reduced models." [4]

III

The construction of a stylistic typology of the sculpture of the Dogon country involves certain methodological problems. The sculpture was invested with meaning by the Dogon themselves, but it cannot be interpreted by a mechanical reference to mythology. Two reservations stated by Lévi-Strauss are in order. He asks if mythic representations correspond to an actual structure that shapes social and religious practices or if they only translate the fixed image by means of which native philosophers give themselves the illusion of stabilizing a reality that eludes them. In reality, mythic activity draws upon collective material bequeathed by preceding generations with modifications that should not be underestimated. The question remains as to what extent this heritage was transmitted in its entirety. Is it the result of a process of simultaneous selection and enrichment or does it possess within itself a coherence with which it is transmitted? Or does it consist of diverse elements belonging to ruined systems which the mind merges and reorganizes into a new system? The coherence of certain systems leads us to believe that they are indeed constructions.

The heritage of ideas and beliefs passed on from generation to generation is

4. I am thinking here of Erwin Panofsky's study "The History of the Theory of Human Proportions as a Reflection of the History of Styles" (reprinted in *Meaning in the Visual Arts*, New York: Doubleday Anchor Books, 1955, pp. 55–107): "Not only is it important to know whether particular artists or periods of art did or did not tend to adhere to a system of proportions, but the how of their mode of treatment is of real significance. For it would be a mistake to assume that theories of proportions *per se* are constantly one and the same. . . . If, in considering the various systems of proportions known to us, we try to understand their meaning rather than their appearance, if we concentrate not so much on the solution arrived at as on the formulation of the problem posed, they will reveal themselves as expressions of the same 'artistic intention' (*Kunstwollen*) that was realized in the buildings, sculptures and paintings of a given period or a given artist. The history of the theory of proportions is the reflection of the history of style; furthermore, since we may understand each other unequivocally when dealing with mathematical formulations, it may even be looked upon as a reflection which often surpasses its original in clarity. One might assert that the theory of proportions expresses the frequently perplexing concept of the *Kunstwollen* in clearer or, a least, more definable fashion than art itself."

not immutable. Some ideas are abandoned or diminish in importance; others are repressed if they perpetuate painful historical memories; still others are stabilized, emphasized, or even reinterpreted. The abandoned ideas leave no trace because there is no information at our disposal to situate them in time. Nevertheless, it seems as if the selection or emphasis of certain mythic elements at the expense of others proceeded along a structural orientation that reestablishes a system similar in form to the preceding one. Thus, when the horse appears in the cosmogony it does not disrupt the etiological system of descent from the granary or the ark but is integrated into that system and carries with it a nuance concerning war (and perhaps the "ritual thief").

Lévi-Strauss has compared *bricolage* on a technical level with mythic activity on an intellectual level.[5] The comparison points out certain characteristics of mythic activity and how it operates. The process has its equivalents in the production of sculpture. In *bricolage*, as in mythic activity, there is ceaseless reconstruction with the same materials. But there are always "ancient purposes called in to play the role of means." Mythic activity elaborates structures "by arranging events or residues of events." This is how the sculptor works: he starts with an inherited inventory of themes, techniques, and formal conventions learned during his apprenticeship. He selects from among them and combines the chosen elements into a sculpture. All of the elements are heavily loaded with meaning, from which they neither can nor should be separated, and they cluster according to affinities or incompatibilities, but they contain a margin of indeterminateness sufficient to authorize their being combined in new constellations.

Inventory of Themes

My central hypothesis is that the sculpture of the Dogon country does not symbolize thought but stimulates it. The three-dimensional ideographs or signs ma-

---

5. The word *bricolage*, as used by Lévi-Strauss, has no precise equivalent in English. A *bricoleur* is "someone who works with his hands and uses devious means compared to those of a craftsman. . . . He is adept at performing a large number of diverse tasks; but, unlike the engineer, he does not subordinate each of them to the availability of raw materials and tools conceived and procured for the purpose of the project. His universe of instruments is closed and the rules of his game are always to make do with 'whatever is at hand,' that is to say with a set of tools and materials which is always finite and is also heterogeneous because what it contains bears no relation to the current project, or indeed to any particular project, but is the contingent result of all the occasions there have been to renew or enrich the stock or to maintain it with the remains of previous constructions or destructions." (*The Savage Mind*, Chicago and London, 1966, pp. 16–17. Originally published as *La Pensée sauvage*, Paris, 1962).

nipulated by the sculptor create new combinations from which myth springs forth. The study of themes (iconographic signs) must be undertaken in relation to the elaboration of a typology. The thematic classification makes it appear that in the material now known to us certain themes are treated exclusively in certain styles. The androgynous figures with raised arms and the horsemen occur in presumed Tellem sculpture (nos. 8, 10, 11, 13, 17, 21, 22, 24, 43, 44) as well as in Dogon sculpture (nos. 19, 23, 46, 47). Other themes are stylistically more limited; cups supported by donkeys and surmounted by a lid with a second figure riding a second donkey appear only in the style of the example shown here (no. 53).

I here limit myself to a simple description of the numerous themes now known to occur in the sculpture of the Dogon country. I have avoided references to myth so as not to pretend to pose a solution to the problem at the beginning.

A. *Figures with Raised Arms*

1. Statistically most numerous are standing human figures, their arms unarticulated by elbows and raised above the head as an extension of the body. They can be subdivided according to differences in the shape of the body and the legs.

> a. In most known examples the body has a human torso (nos. 8, 11, 12, 16, 17, 19, 21, 23).
> b. Sometimes the body has a sinuous shape (no. 25).
> c. The chest may be indicated by a low swelling under the head. The breasts are not differentiated (nos. 17, 21, 23).
> d. The figure may have two differentiated breasts (nos. 11, 12, 16, 19).
> e. Some examples have only one leg shaped roughly like a drumstick (nos. 10, 11, 13).
> f. In others, the legs may be separated by a shallow furrow or otherwise clearly distinct (nos. 12, 16, 17, 21–23).
> g. Most examples in the A group have both hands open with fingers outstretched, but there are rare exceptions in which the right hand, palm forward, is closed (Rietberg Museum, Zurich; Leuzinger, 1967, p. 82, pl. 6).

2. So far as I know, a unique example: a bearded figure with raised arms, no chest articulation, seated with his knees drawn up against his body (no. 18).

3. Some figures have four arms (no. 10) with two additional arms extending downward from the two raised arms and meeting over the abdomen. A female figure on a mask in the Klejman Collection has two raised arms and two additional arms down the sides of the body and distinct from it (University Museum, 1956, p. 58, no. 1-F).

46

Village shrine at Sanga

4. Another unique figure, in the Lazard Collection, is seated, his arms beside his body. On top of his skull are two rods resembling raised arms (Laude, 1964, p. 49, fig. 3).

5. This group consists of superimposed figures, one or both raising their arms. There is a vast number of examples here, which can be grouped as follows:

    a. A figure with a sinuous body, differentiated breasts, and only one leg, superimposed upon what seems to be a head (no. 25).

    b. The upper figure, which is reduced to a head and a single bent leg, stands on the head of a figure with differentiated breasts, a jutting navel, and separated legs (no. 24). Both figures have raised arms.

    c. Two superimposed figures have arms raised in tandem. They are identical except in size; the lower figure is half as large as the upper. Both have a single leg shaped like a drumstick (Lazard Collection).

    d. An upper figure with differentiated breasts and bent, separated legs stands on a lower figure, which is reduced to head, jutting chest, and bent leg extended by a long foot (Lazard Collection).

    e. A figure with raised arms, differentiated breasts, bent and separated legs, stands on the head of a figure whose skull is cleft above the eyes. The lower figure has differentiated breasts, bent and separated legs, and arms extending down the body with hands joined at the groin (Museum of Primitive Art, 1959, pl. 10).

    f. A unique specimen, unusual in its complexity (no. 26). Two upper figures stand on two lower figures, whose heads are joined by an incised plaque. The two lower figures stand on a two-legged plaque that serves as a platform with female symbols incised on the front and male symbols on the back. All four figures have arms down their sides. Chests are represented by a slight swelling that is integrated into the form of the shoulders.

6. The figures in this group raise only one arm.

    a. Sometimes the figure has only one arm, which is an elongation of the body and rises behind the head (no. 14).

    b. Sometimes the left arm alone is raised. The right arm hangs down the side of the body and bends toward the groin (no. 28).

    c. A one-legged figure stands on the head of a figure with bent and separated legs; a single arm elongates both bodies (Hanover Gallery, 1959, fig. 7).

B. *Superimposed Bearded Figures*

There are two examples in this group, which is iconographically distinct and should not be considered a variant of A-5. A bearded figure clasps the ankles of another bearded figure that sits on his shoulders (Laude, 1964, p. 64, fig. 5).

C. *Horsemen*

This group, also numerically important, can be subdivided according to the position of the rider on his mount, his posture, and his gestures.

1. The rider, thrown back, kneels on a quadruped (no. 44).

2. The rider, with differentiated breasts, kneels on a quadruped and leans forward (no. 43).

3. A horseman with differentiated breasts rides bareback and grips his mount with bent knees. He leans back and raises his hands toward the heavens (acquired in Nini in 1935; Leiris and Delange, 1968, p. 229, fig. 261).

4. The horseman is riding a saddled and bridled mount, holding the reins in one hand (nos. 46, 47). One arm is bent. The right fist holds what appears to be a weapon (no. 47). Sometimes the raised arm is a separate piece attached at the shoulder (Museum of Primitive Art, 1959, pl. 13).

D. *Stools with Caryatids*

This large and varied group consists of stools made of two disks joined by a central shaft around which are four caryatids. It can be subdivided into four groups.

1. No figure is seated on the stool. The caryatids are either four single figures or four couples (no. 36) with raised arms and differentiated breasts. In other examples the caryatids are more varied; one specimen, unique so far as I know, has two levels and eight figures (Boussard Collection). Another unique example has only three figures with raised arms. The edges of these stools are always incised with two lines of chevron pattern around the upper disk and one line around the lower disk.

Also belonging to this subgroup, although they are not stools, are sculptures which have a varying number of figures (four to eight) standing around a central column surmounted by a cup (no. 31) or a disk (no. 34).

2. One figure is seated on the stool. The caryatids are figures whose arms hug the body with hands joined below the abdomen (no. 33). The upper disk is joined to the seated figure, male or female. In other examples, the caryatids have been reduced to simple bent shapes (no. 39).

3. A couple is seated on the stool. The man has a quiver on his back. His left arm encircles the shoulders of the woman, who carries a child on her back (no. 37; cf. the example in the Barnes Foundation; Leiris and Delange, 1968, pp. 224–25, figs. 253, 254).

A possible variant of the D group consists of couples seated on simple, unworked columns. The man's left arm encircles the woman's shoulders (Rietberg Museum; Leuzinger, 1967, p. 83, pl. 7). But the couples sometimes stand, either joined only by the plinth or, as in the preceding examples, with the man's left arm encircling the woman's shoulders (Musée National des Arts Africains et Océaniens; Lem, 1948, pl. 6).

E. *Women with Children*
This group can be subdivided as follows:
1. The woman is standing and carries the child on her lower left arm (no. 55) or on her left hip (Museum of Primitive Art).
2. The woman is standing. Under each of her arms, which hang down the body, is a standing child (Laude, 1968, slide no. 33).
3. The woman is standing and carrying a child on her back. In another example, she is carrying two children (no. 30). In both of these examples, the woman carries a cup on her head.
4. The woman is kneeling and carrying a child on her back (no. 58).
5. The woman is kneeling and suckling two children. There is a crocodile in relief on her back (Rasmussen Collection).
6. The woman is kneeling and carrying a child on each arm and another on her back (no. 57). In another example she carries two children on her back and a third on her left arm (no. 56).
7. The woman is kneeling and holding a child on her knees.

F. *Figures Covering Their Faces*
This is a diversified group. Some are sitting (no. 3; another in the Rasmussen Collection). Some are standing (example from Yougo in the Musée de l'Homme).

G. *Women Grinding Millet*
Several examples constitute a rather homogeneous thematic group which varies only stylistically (examples in the Charles Ratton and Henri Kamer Collections).

H. *Women Bearing Vessels on Their Heads*
This large group contains only a few notable variables. Some of the women bend

50

their elbows forward and hold their hands to their ears (Laude, 1964, p. 65, fig. 7), some hold the cup, and some hold their hands on their thighs (no. 32).

I. *Donkeys Bearing Cups*
This group is stylistically homogeneous. The lid of the cup is surmounted by a second donkey which in turn is surmounted by a human figure (no. 53). An example in the Musée de l'Homme has a female figure kneeling on the lid. An example in the Museum of Primitive Art has on the lid of the cup a figure seated on a stool supported by caryatids and grinding millet in a mortar (Laude, 1964, p. 64, fig. 6).

J. *Musicians*
I know of only two examples, which differ stylistically: a figure who appears to be playing a lute, formerly in the Kamer Collection, and two seated xylophone players in the Museum of Primitive Art (Laude, 1964, p. 64, fig. 6).

K. *Dogs*
Several figures of dogs are known (no. 54). An example in the Museum of Primitive Art has a small cup on its back; on each flank is a pair of figures in relief, their arms at their sides (Laude, 1964, p. 65, fig. 8).

L. *Quadruped-shaped Troughs or Benches*
This large group comprises troughs or long benches in the shape of a quadruped which is hard to identify but may be a horse. Some examples have figures covering their faces in relief on the lid and herringbone patterns and rectangles incised on the flanks. No. 51 is engraved with herringbone pattern only on the legs and the top, which has a lid that opens on two hinges to reveal a small cavity inside. Other specimens have no legs and are not hollow inside; no. 50 has figures in relief on the sides, and no. 49 has herringbone pattern on the neck and sides.

M. *Figures Bending from the Waist*
Two examples are known of figures bending from the waist. Neither has a base. The arms hang down the sides. The head is turned slightly toward the left. The first example has a leg shaped like a drumstick (no. 5); the second, in the N. Richard Miller Collection, has two distinct legs.

N. *Mirror-Image*
A unique object (no. 15) is surmounted by a bearded head and the remains of two

raised arms. Beneath the head is another head upside down, a mirror image of the first. Beneath the skull of the lower head is a standing figure flanked on either side by a taller standing figure.

O. *Plaque*
Also unique is an openwork plaque surmounted by a profile head (no. 64). Cut into the plaque are three standing figures, with arms hanging down and hands joined on the abdomen. The central figure wears a metal bell around his neck. Above the figures is a crocodile in relief on the front and a snake on the back.

P. *Aproned Figure*
Another unique object is a bearded figure, arms hanging down and bent at the elbow (no. 42). He wears an apron around his waist, which is adorned with geometric signs. On his right shoulder is a bent tool, perhaps an adze.

Q. *Standing Figures*
This group consists of works stylistically very heterogeneous and thematically unified only by their posture. They are male and female figures, standing, with their arms hanging down. No. 60 has a peculiarity which is unique so far as I know: a stone incorporated into the torso.

Themes and Forms

The relationship of themes to forms poses certain problems. Some themes, such as figures with raised arms and horsemen, were treated in practically all known styles; others, such as dogs and cup-bearing donkeys, are stylistically homogeneous. The themes themselves are extraordinarily diverse as are the formal systems conceived and elaborated by the Dogon sculptor. Such thematic and stylistic diversity is exceptional in Black Africa.

Themes have structural elements which must be identified, and forms inversely seem to have thematic meaning. Dogon art is an art of the sign. The sculptor has no desire to imitate the particular appearance of an object, a human figure for example, but to reproduce the object as the deity designed it in the beginning. These signs, however, have considerable multiplicity of meaning and can be combined in numerous ways. They are instruments of knowledge, exploring reality without fixing it in concepts, as well as means of action that contribute to the ordering and organization of reality.

Themes themselves can be polymorphous; they may be expressed, made concrete, by a variety of formal structures. In attempting classifications, we must bear in mind this double series of variables: the multiplicity of meaning attached to the sign and the ability of themes to be expressed by different formal structures. This is fundamental in the thinking of the Dogon people and is true of all systems of knowledge, both *closed* (knowledge achieved through the progressive revelations of initiation) and *open* (knowledge explored with the help of new depths of thought created by signs and new combinations of signs).

Formal systems are simultaneously relative to and independent of canonic meanings and institutional functions. The Dogon artist does not clothe ideas or concepts in forms; he does not translate ideas or interpret them with a play of lines and masses, rhythms and volumes. He thinks directly *with* forms, *in* forms. Moreover, style is not determined by the elements of his culture; it is a component of that culture. The sculptures are archives in the strictest sense of the word, and they must not be read as if they were pictorial lectures. They must be interpreted in the context in which they were produced.

Let us now examine the broad characteristics that would permit an initial classification (admittedly inadequate) of these systems and modes of formal arrangement.

The Style of Yayé

Three works make up this group. The first is a relatively intact androgynous figure excavated at Yayé, near Mopti, in 1935 by Denise Paulme (Leiris and Delange, 1968, pp. 218–19, figs. 247, 248). The second is the head of an old man, probably a fragment of a figure similar to the first, discovered by Langlois in a village in the Banani cluster (Langlois, 1954, fig. 8). Another work, found in the village of Nandoli, is badly eroded by time and reveals only an outline with certain allusive indications. Of these three works, we might say that the sculpture is still enveloped in its original material. As simple as they may appear, however, all three manifest a high degree of sophistication in the way the artist has abstracted certain elements to support not a sensory apprehension of the figure but a profound intellectual vision.

Figures with Raised Arms

These works are coated with sacrificial patina. They were carved from a single surface of a tree trunk, but they vary in relation to the original material. They range from figures whose forms exist only in low relief on a flat surface (nos. 11, 13) to those freed from this background (no. 23). Legs may be part of the same cylinder as the torso and separated only by a shallow incision or a deeper furrow, but when the sculptural volumes are full and rich the limbs are distinct and no longer merged.

Works in the first group are thin and elongated. They consist of a single volume with an undifferentiated, often unworked, back. The sculptor has penetrated the density of the wood by cutting into the surface of the principal volume. He has interrupted its verticality (although not on all of its surfaces) with a system of notches that define and limit secondary volumes, which are not allowed to expand forcefully. Each of the forms thus appears to be backed onto a flat surface that may extend beyond it and on which it has the general appearance of a relief.

The shape of the wood does not determine the form of the figure. Nor does the theme dictate its slenderness or smoothness, since the same theme is often treated in sculpture with richer and fuller volumes. Slenderness and smoothness thus appear to be elements of style. Moreover, those figures whose head and bust are set against the back plane formed by the prolongation of the raised arms can be distinguished according to whether the legs are distinct or undifferentiated, separate or together, straight or bent.

These distinctions raise two fundamental problems. Is the back plane that supports these figures homologous to the tall blade that tops the Great Masks? The plane of the raised arms is subject to certain variations, but it is always present.

In terms of the suggestion furnished by the blade-mask, the figures most likely should be seen as integral with their back plane. But the plane was opened up, emptied out, and thus it depicts the two raised arms joined by the open hands. Next the arms were further particularized so that the plane survives only to hip level (nos. 11, 24). The original meaning of the plane was probably forgotten with the development of the individual arms.

The problem of the figures with raised arms and the blade-masks is connected with the problem of the articulation of the human body, which is explained in a myth of origin. The original eight genii, the *nommos*, were water spirits and had sinuous bodies and limbs. One of them, the blacksmith, descended to earth in an ark, bringing tools, seeds, and animals as well as human ancestors with him. The

54

ark landed with a brutal impact, and under the weight of his mace and his anvil, the limbs of the blacksmith broke at the knees, shoulders, and elbows. Thus man can work (and dance). The myth may provide an insight into the interrupted contours and undifferentiated surfaces of the carved figures.

In some figures, the body is represented as a supple and sinuous structure behind which we see a flat back support (no. 25). Others are arched forward or backward with no suggestion of sinuosity; the curve is extreme. These arched figures appear also as caryatids supporting stools, but whereas the stool exhibits interpenetrations of interior and exterior space, the caryatid figure always has a smooth back. The limbs, however, are differentiated and slightly separated. The figure is placed against a back plane clearly visible from the side, and this back plane is maintained for all objects of this type (no. 36). It appears occasionally on caryatids supporting stools on which a figure in the round is seated. On stools on which couples or androgynous figures are seated, however, the caryatid figures are treated in relief, but with three-dimensional depth (nos. 33, 37).

We see that the back plane is used only for figures with raised arms, but it is not always present. In some examples, it is suggested only by a cursory indication and in others is completely absent. As the back plane tends to disappear, the legs become separate and distinct. The arms may end at the hips. In certain examples, the legs are represented by a cylinder that prolongs the torso or by a base in the shape of a truncated cone. Water spirits (*nommos*) are sometimes described as having only one leg in the shape of a drumstick or a fish (no. 5). We now have another work in the same style as no. 5, from the same studio if not the same hand, which depicts a *nommo* with two undifferentiated legs; we can thus dismiss the interpretation claiming that the separation and individualization of the limbs are due to progress in skill, to an acquired mastery.

Tactile and Visual

Those works which exhibit a certain degree of sensory realism offer a synthetic image of man. Their contours suffice to identify them—the curves and breaks of the surface, the full volumes mitigate the absence of figurative details but force the observer to apprehend the work to the exclusion of analysis or any illustrational sense of form.

Other works are more intellectually conceived and appeal to the visual rather than the tactile sense. These works may be exposed to view, either occasionally, for funerary rites, or permanently. Once out of the sanctuary they recede mate-

55

rially from the officiant or faithful to whom they are no longer linked by the intimate complicity encouraged by handling. This group is less homogeneous. In these works, strong accents are not enveloped and controlled by the surface but are clearly distinct and stabilized, forming a succession of lateral beats that oppose the rhythm of the primary volume. Space is conquered through the balancing of masses and the tension between contrasting solids and between solids and voids. Although primacy has been conferred on the sense of sight, these works nevertheless reveal a certain feeling for tactile values, but it is controlled and integrated into more abstract formal systems.

New kinds of tensions are created by straight lines that laterally articulate the curved surfaces. Incisions are no longer restricted to the contour but enter into the mass itself. The sculptor may reveal his presence by cutting deeply into the surface with a plane or a void. The figures in this group vary considerably in style and theme, and the same theme may be treated in several styles. The works themselves can be classified into two large groups. Those which exhibit a tendency toward narrative and figurative ambiguity or duality make up the first. The second can in turn be subdivided into those characterized by an analytical and hieratic design and those exhibiting a geometricizing and monumental character in association with a system of combining forms in a system of "montage."

The figures with raised arms and the sculptures that exhibit sensory realism generally refer to events with equivalents in myth. They concern spirits or heroes caught in the act that defines them. There is no ambiguity; the sculpture expresses a reality, but it is a reality with no equivalent in daily life. Some kneeling figures can be connected to a mythical act or represent a religious gesture or ritual pose. The ambiguity is not real; it is our lack of information that makes us hesitate.

Figures of women grinding millet, on the other hand, capture the action and posture of all housewives at a routine task. But they are also images and substitutes of the *hogon* whose life, according to myth, is identified with the growing of millet. Thus, they are prototypes of all housewives who grind grain in their mortars and turn it into food and of the *hogon* whose material and spiritual life is closely bound up with the germination and growth of grains. Sculptures of this type are involved in earthly time, arrested at a meaningful moment, and in the total time of myth. Within earthly or human time, they assert a generally recognizable but not symbolic image of an everyday reality given value by its meaning. Within mythic time, they assert an absolute and inalterable truth, one of the essential values of material and spiritual life. This duality permits a

56

Dancers, drummers and singers from cave at Bongo

freer expression of movement, notably with the theme of the horseman. The enrichment of thematic elements seems to accompany a modification of stylistic formulas.

This duality can be assumed by legendary if not historic events, where the emphasis is more on the human aspect. Figures that represent an old man perched on the shoulders of another old man (Laude, 1971, pp. 130–31, figs. 100, 101) refer to a migration myth. Arou, the youngest of the brothers from whom the Dogon claim their descent, climbed onto the shoulders of his brother, Dyon, to look for a country in which to settle. The representation of Arou on the shoulders of his brother marks a beginning: the settlement of the Dogon, the organization of society, the distribution of political and religious powers. Yet whatever its position in the context of what precedes it, this beginning does not inaugurate a chronological history. It confers authenticity and reality on a social and religious system which itself reproduces an archetypal situation.

Works that exhibit hieratic tendencies are not characterized by the absence of all curved contours. A rigid core encloses the work within an ideal block whose secondary forms do not extend beyond its limits. It is as if the original block had been reduced to a geometric volume before being carved. The sculptor conceives the original block in three dimensions. Following more or less complex formulas, he combines specific elements to construct veritable edifices that enclose all three dimensions and allow interpenetrations of internal and external space. In some, the cylinder seems to be the result of an abstraction released from the original tree trunk. But not all sculptures of this type are the same; the relation of the sculpture to the original cylinder varies. Neither the nature of the original block nor the theme plays an important part in the definition of the stylistic formula; they constitute conditions that direct stylistic tendencies but do not determine them. Certain formulas permit volumes greater autonomy; in others, the tendency of forms to expand is more controlled.

Works in which the sculptor hollows out the mass, saving subsidiary details for its interior, show a tendency toward fretwork carving. Depending on how he treats the block, the sculptor can deal more or less with the interpenetration of spaces, particularly in the *imago mundi* stools (nos. 33, 36, 37). Openwork sculpture is favored but not determined by the geometricizing tendency, which, associated with the treatment of blocks, reveals an attraction for interior spaces. This system has also been exploited in certain works that tend toward the hieratic (the xylophone players), but here it is the design that limits the development of the volumes and creates tensions that prevent the forms from expanding beyond

58

the external armature. In works in the geometricizing tendency, on the other hand, the expansion of forms around the internal core is greater. The formula is based on the volumes themselves, taken as true plastic units.

Such a tendency leads to a certain monumentality, despite the small size of the sculptures. Such works as the one in the Museum of Primitive Art, representing the descent of the Word as a *nommo* with raised arms entering into the cleft skull of the *hogon*, are examples, as well as the splendid figures of women with vessels on their heads (Laude, 1964, p. 65, fig. 7). They are monumental partly because the forms are clearly defined and autonomous, partly because broken rhythms mitigate the discontinuity introduced by the projection of animated forms in a motionless entity, and finally because the result is a true "montage" of all the elements in a single unified form.

Works of this stylistic type include the couples seated on *imago mundi* stools (no. 37). Sometimes the two figures are compressed into a single androgynous one (no. 33). In other examples the man has one arm around the woman's shoulders. Here the elements are dictated by meaning; the couple is eternal. This is not an illustration of an event but a complete recapitulation of cosmogony, of history, and the organization of society. These sculptures are commemorative (they recall the events involved in the creation of the world and the organization of society), etiological (they explain the system of the world and the social and political structures of the Dogon), and didactic (they teach the system of the world and those structures). The sculptor replaces the idea of movement with the idea of "montage" or combination in three dimensions. Movement would imply time and would thus alter the very nature of the necessary and intangible order. But this order is life; it is not inert. It conditions and regulates spiritual and physical life, cosmic and earthly life, mythic and social life.

We may end this cursory description by mentioning a double aspect of "sculptural rhythm." The vitalistic aspect, expressed in rich and full volumes, in spatial expansion, is based on the identification of man (especially the *hogon*) with a grain of millet. It is joined to an ordering, regulating aspect, expressed in the creation of conventional forms (abstract signs and rhythmic sequences) based on the system of classifications ruling the relations of human beings with one another, of human beings and other animate beings, and of biological and cosmic correspondences.

Verticality, the spiral or broken line, and symmetry are sometimes, though not always, combined in one and the same work, but any one of them may be emphasized and appear as the dominant element. All three are joined to ideas or values rooted in the ideological substratum. They are, moreover, bound up with rhythmic formulas that can be correlated with ideological tendencies.

Verticality dominates in the figures with raised arms, and it is defined as an expressive, meaningful element. A double movement is expressed: a vertical thrust of man toward the heavenly world and the descent of the spirit into the earthly world.

The spiral or broken line is more particularly associated with the latter movement and refers to the fall of the original blacksmith and the ark, carrying technology, human ancestors, animals, and seeds. Enveloping the structure or limited to its surface decoration, the spiral or broken line recalls the vibration of speech, water, light. It is related also to the movement of the thread in the weft and the shape of the serpent Lébé, into which the *nommo* was transformed when he was sacrificed to the soil in order to purify the earth after the original act of incest committed by Dyougou Serou.

The proliferation of meanings always leads back to the central notion of vibratory movement, of growth, and of creative life. Verticality defines a directional thrust rather than a movement itself; the spiral or broken line encloses space more completely. It is also more dynamic and permits clearer oppositions and contrasts of forms, as well as the animation of component volumes. In those works where the spiral or broken line is integrated into the sculpture rather than applied to the surface, we have references to the breaking of limbs and the articulation of the human body.

Symmetry involves the notions of twinship and bisexuality. Figures of twins or couples refer to conceptions about the powers of generation and the life cycle. The vitalism inherent in these ideas arises from a dynamism, whose sculptural expression does not, however, reveal a burning instinct to invade every activity of life and consciousness, but is tempered by the ordering aspect of rhythm.

In a sense, we can say that the principles of twinship and bisexuality contained within themselves the remedies to the brutal and uncontrolled expansion of the conceptions they convey and transmit. They prepared the way for the initial classification or, more exactly, differentiation, since the bisexuality of human prototypes turned out to be inconvenient and a cause of disorder. In other words, symmetry tends to mitigate the effects of intemperate dynamism encouraged by the vitalism inherent in these themes. It suggests a classification, an order. It tends to repress dynamic power with ordering power.

Women on their way to market

Friday market at Sanga

Farmers on the rocks at Kamba

Pounding onions at Sanga

THE CATALOGUE

1. Bracelet with figure of Dyougou Serou hiding his face. Brass, *cire perdue*. Diameter 4 in. (10 cm.)

DYOUGOU SEROU

The god Amma created the earth from a lump of clay. The body of the earth was feminine; its sexual organ was an anthill and its clitoris a termite hill. The lonely creator approached the earth, desiring sexual intercourse, but the earth was unwilling; the termite hill rose up in resistance, revealing its masculinity. Amma cut it down and then had intercourse with the excised earth. Because the latter was an unwilling partner, this was a breach in the order of the universe. The offspring of this union was Dyougou Serou, who, having no wife, committed incest with his mother. As a result of his incestuous act, Dyougou Serou was endowed with the gift of the first word, the earliest, most primitive language. To rectify the impurity caused by Dyougou Serou's misdeed, Amma decided to create human beings directly, without further union with the earth. Dyougou Serou is shown hiding his face in his hands in shame for his misdeed.

2. Figurine. This figure does not hide its face but holds its head in its hands. It may belong to another sequence of the Dyougou Serou myth or to another myth entirely. Brass, *cire perdue*. Height 2¾ in. (7 cm.)

3. Figurine of Dyougou Serou hiding his face. Wood with sacrificial patina. Height 5½ in. (14 cm.). Publ. Leiris and Delange, 1968, p. 223, fig. 252

NOMMOS AND FIGURES WITH RAISED ARMS

The earth having been excised—that is to say feminized by the removal of the male element, the termite hill clitoris—Amma was once again united with her. The offspring were a pair of *nommos* and then four other *nommo* couples. Each *nommo* was bisexual, but the female element dominated in some, the male element in others. The bodies of the *nommos* were sinuous, supple as water, and without joints. Each had a single leg, in the shape of a drumstick or a fish. The first *nommo* pair constituted the Primordial Couple. The four other pairs became the eight heads of lineage for all human beings. They set sail on an ark that descended from the sky to the earth. But before the journey, one of them was sacrificed to the heavens and his body scattered in five parts over the earth, at the four points of the compass and into the center of the earth, where the genital was transformed into a crocodile. A second *nommo* was sacrificed when the ark landed, in order to purify the earth. He was transformed into the serpent Lébé and, after three days, became the leader of the Dogon migration.

The theme of raised arms is related to a number of mythic elements. The *nommo* ancestor lifts his arms to the sky for the rain of forgiveness. He is also represented during his sacrifice, crucified on a tree with his hands above his head.

The *nommo*, as bearer of the word, is sometimes represented as descending into the skull of a *hogon*.

4. Standing *nommo* with distinct, bent legs. The nose is serpent-shaped and the mouth wide. On the upper torso are rectangles crossed by diagonals and on the abdomen a herringbone pattern. Bells hang from the wrists. Iron. Height 8¼ in. (21 cm.)

5. One-legged *nommo* leaning backward. Tellem style. Wood. Height 16 in. (40.5 cm.). Length 26¼ in. (66.5 cm.). Publ. Laude, 1964, p. 49, fig. 4

6. *Nommo* caught at the instant of metamorphosis into a crocodile. Iron. Height 3½ in. (8.4 cm.). Length 4¾ in. (12 cm.)

7. Head of a *nommo*. This may have been part of a *hogon*'s scepter. The nose of the *nommo* is serpent-shaped, the mouth wide, the ears shaped like horseshoes. The herringbone pattern on the handle is an allusion to the serpent Lébé (in whose being the *hogon* participates) and to a complex of related images, including the movement of thread in the weft. Wood. Height 13½ in. (34.3 cm.).

8. *Nommo* with raised arms. Tellem style. This unique piece is characterized by the extreme abstraction of the face. The meaning of the work is revealed by the two raised arms and the egg-shaped head, without indication of features. On the back is a second *nommo* with distinct arms and legs. Wood with sacrificial patina. Height 18½ in. (47 cm.)

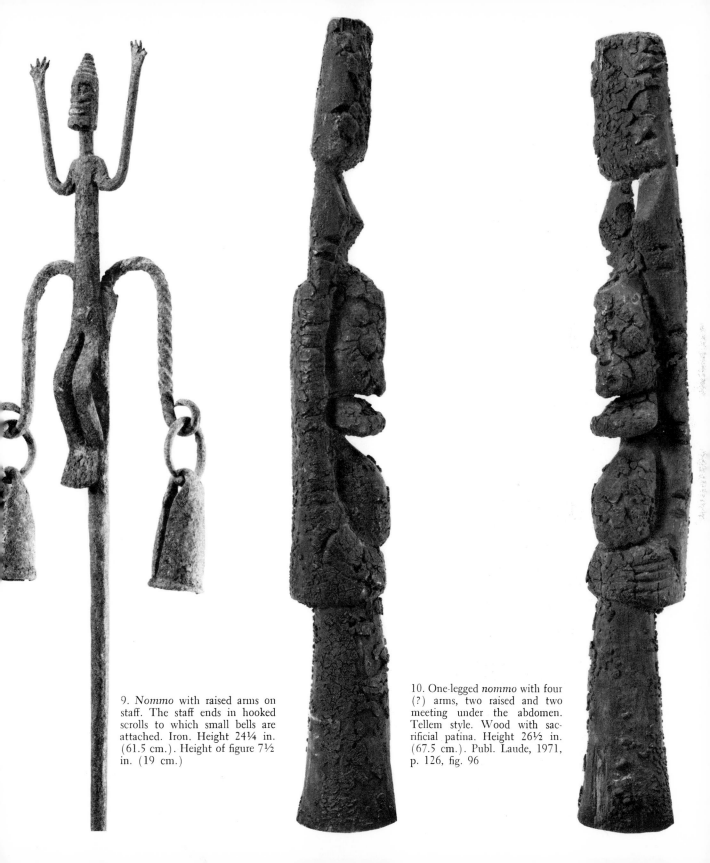

9. *Nommo* with raised arms on staff. The staff ends in hooked scrolls to which small bells are attached. Iron. Height 24¼ in. (61.5 cm.). Height of figure 7½ in. (19 cm.)

10. One-legged *nommo* with four (?) arms, two raised and two meeting under the abdomen. Tellem style. Wood with sacrificial patina. Height 26½ in. (67.5 cm.). Publ. Laude, 1971, p. 126, fig. 96

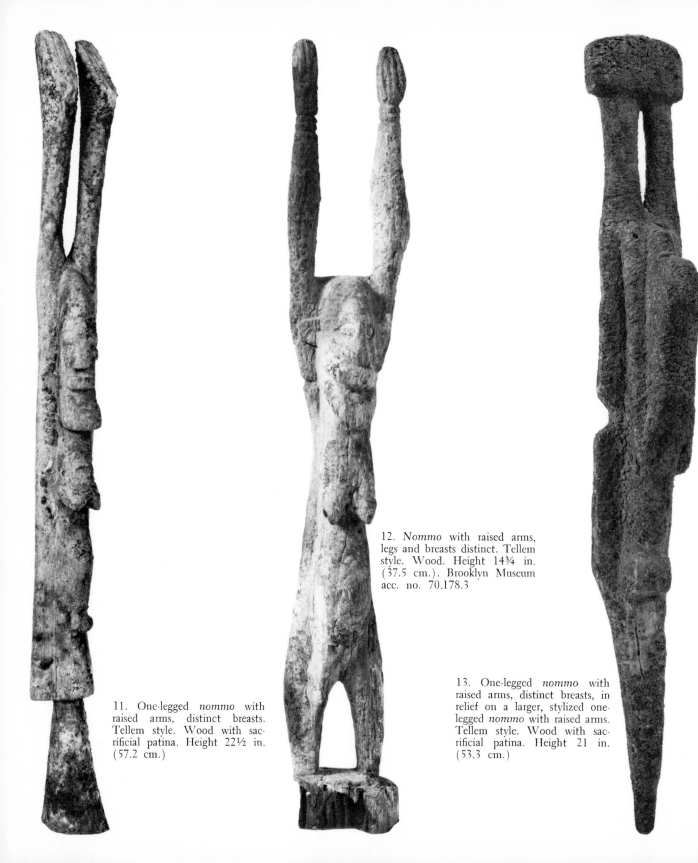

11. One-legged *nommo* with raised arms, distinct breasts. Tellem style. Wood with sacrificial patina. Height 22½ in. (57.2 cm.)

12. *Nommo* with raised arms, legs and breasts distinct. Tellem style. Wood. Height 14¾ in. (37.5 cm.). Brooklyn Museum acc. no. 70.178.3

13. One-legged *nommo* with raised arms, distinct breasts, in relief on a larger, stylized one-legged *nommo* with raised arms. Tellem style. Wood with sacrificial patina. Height 21 in. (53.3 cm.)

14. *Nommo* with one raised arm, legs and breasts distinct. Tellem style. Wood with sacrificial patina. Height 17⅛ in. (43.3 cm.). Brooklyn Museum acc. no. 70.178.4

15. Composite figure carved in high relief. The arms originally joined the body at the level of the ears or above the head. Other works in the same style were allegedly discovered in Ende or in Kani Bonzon. This piece is related to the complex of meanings associated with the theme of raised arms, but its precise meaning is obscure. Wood, badly eroded. Height 16½ in. (42 cm.). Publ. Palais Granvelle, 1958, pl. V, no. 34

16. *Nommo* with raised arms, legs and breasts distinct. Tellem style. Wood. Height 30½ in. (77.5 cm.). Brooklyn Museum acc. no. 70.178.5

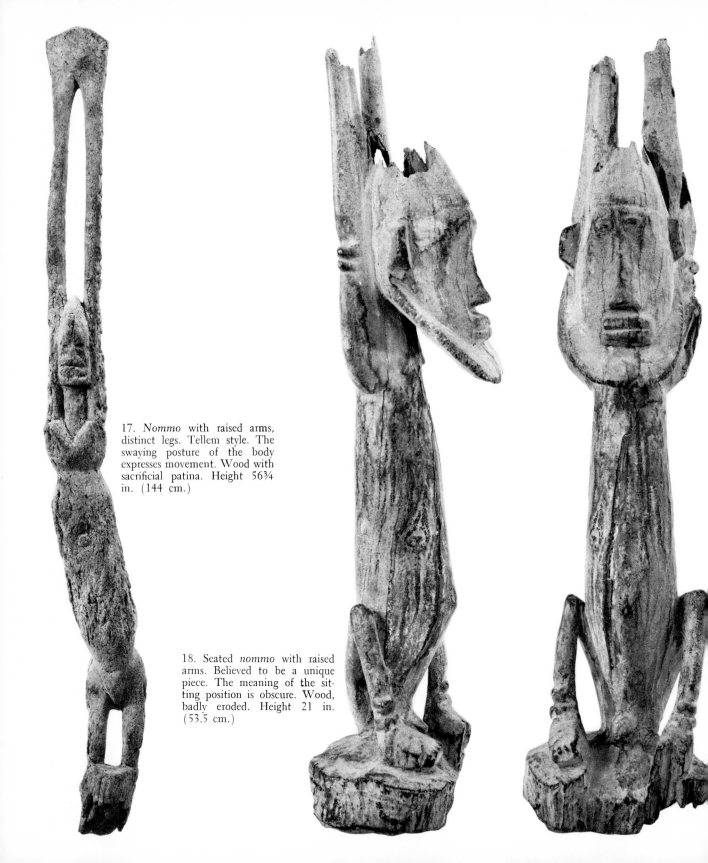

17. *Nommo* with raised arms, distinct legs. Tellem style. The swaying posture of the body expresses movement. Wood with sacrificial patina. Height 56¾ in. (144 cm.)

18. Seated *nommo* with raised arms. Believed to be a unique piece. The meaning of the sitting position is obscure. Wood, badly eroded. Height 21 in. (53.5 cm.)

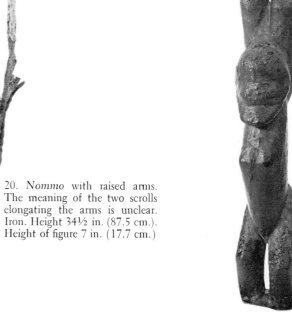

20. *Nommo* with raised arms. The meaning of the two scrolls elongating the arms is unclear. Iron. Height 34½ in. (87.5 cm.). Height of figure 7 in. (17.7 cm.)

21. *Nommo* with raised arms, distinct legs. Tellem style. Wood. Height 17 in. (43 cm.)

19. *Nommo* with raised arms, distinct breasts. Scarifications on breasts and abdomen. Wood, badly eroded. Height 43 in. (109 cm.). Publ. Meauzé, 1967, p. 154, fig. 1

22. Four joined *nommos* with raised arms. Tellem style. Each *nommo* probably represents a couple. Wood with sacrificial patina. Height 19½ in. (49.5 cm.). Width 7 in. (17.8 cm.)

23. *Nommo* with raised arms, distinct legs. Four bracelets on each arm. Wood. Height 55 in. (140 cm.)

SUPERIMPOSED FIGURES

These works depict the descent of the *nommo* with raised arms into the skull of a figure who is probably the head of the line of *hogons*. The figure into whom the spirit descends is sometimes depicted with female attributes, an echo of the bisexuality of the *nommo*. In some examples, the cranium is split above the brow ridge to indicate the removal of the braincase and thus the suppression of obstacles that would prevent communication between the spirit and the mind it momentarily possesses. The ritual equivalent is the shaving of hair at the enthronement of a *hogon*. We may also have here a reference to the quest for ataractic states, as among the Bambara, where they are symbolized by an ox skull (such ideas can also be found in Pharaonic Egypt).

These sculptures, however, are not depictions of abstract ideas. The *nommo* descends materially into the mind of the *hogon* in order to possess it concretely, either in the form of the serpent Lébé, in whom the *hogon* participates, or in the form of a human figure with raised arms.

24. *Nommo*, reduced to a head and a single bent leg, descending into the skull of a *hogon* with female attributes. Tellem style. The raised arms, shared by both figures, signify that they are of the same essence or that the communion between them is complete. Wood with sacrificial patina. Height 20½ in. (52 cm.)

25. *Nommo* with raised arms, distinct breasts, and a serpent's body terminated by a foot descending into the head of a *hogon*. Tellem style. Wood. Height 37¾ in. (96 cm.)

26. Two-legged plaque supporting a *nommo* couple, their heads joined by a small bridge, with another such couple superimposed above them. In relief on the front of the plaque are male symbols, on the back female ones. Although this work is thematically close to the "descent of the word" examples, there may be an allusion here to another myth. Wood. Height 45½ in. (115.5 cm.)

27. One-legged *nommo*, raising one arm, on a staff. Iron. Height 18¾ in. (47.6 cm.)

28. *Nommo* with distinct legs raising its left arm. In all likelihood, this is a depiction of a *nommo* being resurrected. The form of the arms and chest recalls the superstructures of certain *kanaga* masks (which represent, according to Griaule, the hand of the god). Wood with sacrificial patina. Height 24½ in. (62.2 cm.)

29. Carved stone block with six figures in relief. Two *nommos* (?) on each side and one member of the Primordial Couple (?) at each end. Soft stone. Height 8½ in. (21.5 cm.). Width 5½ in. (14 cm.)

FIGURES CARRYING BOWLS ON THEIR HEADS

To defend their mother the earth against further approaches by their eldest brother, Dyougou Serou, the *nommos* descended to earth and entered into the anthill, the genital from which they had been born. These *nommos* were the heads of the eight lineages of humanity. After some time an obscure instinct led Dyougou Serou to the anthill occupied by the *nommos*. On his head, as protection against the sun, he wore the wooden bowl from which he ate his food. Placing his feet in the anthill, the orifice of the earthly womb, he slowly sank into it as though reversing the process of birth. Thus he was liberated from his earthly condition (Griaule, 1965, pp. 25–26).

Sculptures of figures with bowls on their heads may allude to this sequence of the myth. However, they possess formal determinants that would permit us to identify them as *nommos*, or, more precisely, as the Primordial Couple: the horseshoe-shaped ear, the cylindrical articulation of the chin, and the child or children on the back. Other pieces are more complex and represent an image of the world: four or eight figures cluster around a central column with a small cup rather than a disk on their heads. These pieces can be grouped together without, however, connecting them with the mythic sequence related above.

30. Standing woman, knees bent, arms at her sides, hands joined under the abdomen. She has two children, a male and a female, on her back and a hemispherical bowl on her head. Labret in the lower lip. Wood. Height 15½ in. (39.4 cm.)

31. Eight *nommos* seated around a column that supports a round cup. All have distinct breasts and legs, arms at their sides, with hands joined below the abdomen. All wear labrets in the lower lip. Wood with traces of sacrificial patina. Height 18½ in. (47 cm.)

32. Kneeling woman, arms at her sides, hands resting on the thighs. On the chest are vestiges of herringbone pattern. Labret in the lower lip. On her head, a bowl supported by eight arches, a simplification of eight *nommos* with raised arms. Wood. Height 14 in. (35.5 cm.)

STOOLS AND SEATED FIGURES

According to the Dogon cosmogony described by Griaule in *Masques dogons* (1938), the earth and the sky are two disks linked at their centers by a tree—the *axis mundi*. The figures placed at the four cardinal points around these disks recall the four pairs of *nommo* twins. The herringbone pattern makes concrete a number of related images: the vibration of light, water, speech, the fall of the ark of the blacksmith, and finally the serpent Lébé.

Although they are theoretically the thrones of the *hogons*, these stools are never used for sitting. They represent a complete image of the world as it was created. On certain two-level examples, like that in the Broussard Collection, a complete tale of the creation is developed on each of the eight caryatids.

Isolated figures who can be identified as *hogons*, thanks to certain indications (beard, headdress, etc.), are sometimes seated on these stools. The caryatids are *nommos* with raised arms in the Tellem style, which is not the style of the seated figure. When a couple is represented sitting on the stool, the caryatids are not in the style of the two seated figures, but this time it is not a Tellem style either.

The couple is the Primordial Couple, born before the four other *nommo* couples. Seated on the stool supported by the eight *nommos* from whom all who occupy the Dogon country descend, the couple probably makes manifest not only the existence of the Primordial Couple but also that of the supreme authority. Thus these seats probably refer to the social and political structure of the Dogon country, which is federative: power on a local level is delegated to village *hogons*—aged men who are responsible for those places in which their temporal and spiritual authority is in effect. The supreme *hogon*, chosen at an early age, retains political power over the whole federation. Denise Paulme has rightly pointed out that the supreme *hogon* should be classified among the divine kings so numerous in Black Africa.

The profound structure of the myth serves to explain and maintain the political structure, which draws its legitimacy from being founded on an original order conceived and planned by the god when he created the world. The *imago mundi* stools constitute archives, which we must read for the information they give about the political organization of the Dogon country. We must remember that the mind of the Dogon people is a figurative one, expressed through forms rather than words or concepts.

Certain formal and stylistic peculiarities create problems. The stylistic difference between the seated figures and those that play the role of caryatids suggests two strata of population; the styles in which the two types of figures are treated would thus be formal determinants permitting us to identify the populations to which the figures refer. The presence of the *nommos* with raised arms probably indicates that the tellem were there first, as occupiers and "masters of the soil," mediating between it and the new inhabitants.

33. Woman sitting on a cylindrical stool and four figures. Her horseshoe-shaped ears identify her as one of the Primordial Couple. She has a quiver on her back and holds an unidentified object. She wears a headdress similar to those worn by the Peuls. On each arm is a set of four bracelets and another set of three, which indicates her bisexuality: *three* is the *male* number, *four* the *female* number. She probably represents a contraction of the Primordial Couple into a single person. The four figures who support her are in a style similar to those supporting the cup in no. 31. Wood. Height 23 in. (58.4 cm.)

35. *Hogon* stool consisting of two disks connected by a central post, three *nommo* couples with raised arms and distinct breasts and legs, and a curved plaque on which appears a crocodile in high relief. Two rows of chevron pattern around the top disk and one row around the lower disk. Wood. Height 12½ in. (31.8 cm.)

34. Four standing figures with distinct breasts and arms at their sides supporting a disk. Wood with sacrificial patina. Height 20 in. (51 cm.)

36. *Hogon* stool consisting of two disks connected by a central post and four *nommo* couples with raised arms. Two rows of herringbone pattern around the top disk and one row around the lower. Wood. Height 14 in. (35.5 cm.)

37. Primordial Couple seated on an *imago mundi* stool supported by four figures. The man's right arm is around the woman's neck and his hand touches her right breast; his left hand is on his genital. The woman's hands rest on her thighs. He has an empty quiver on his back and she has a child on hers. He has a trapezoid-shaped beard, she a labret in the shape of a truncated cone with a copper ring around its base. The woman wears four horseshoe-shaped copper rings on each ear (four is the number of femininity) and the man has three rings in each of his (the number of masculinity). Both have arrow-shaped noses that continue the crest of the headgear. The four caryatid figures, arms at their sides and hands crossed below the abdomen, are in a completely different style.

This piece poses a number of questions. The shapes of the noses and ears are more or less identical with those of the *nommo* head in no. 7. Furthermore, the presence of the quiver places the man in the category of hunter or warrior, and the beard identifies him as a chieftain. The presence of the copper-ringed labret in the woman's lip is more difficult to interpret. This motif is not exclusive to the sculpture of the Dogon country; it occurs on Baule sculpture and masks, on soapstone figurines of the Kissi, and on ancestor figures of the Oron-Ibibio. In the twisted form in which it appears on the couple in the Barnes Foundation, the motif is analogous to the false beard on Pharaonic masks that identified the dead sovereign with Osiris. Without pressing the point, we may note that here at least are two elements common to Pharaonic and Dogon sculpture: the arm around the woman's neck and the labret similar in shape to the false beard of the Pharaoh. Moreover, the dismemberment of the *nommo* and the scattering of its body over the earth recall the fate of Osiris.

The headgear worn by both man and woman is similar to that still worn by the Peuls, whom we know to have been antagonists of the Dogon. The edge of the seat is not decorated with a herringbone pattern and thus does not partake of the ancestral Lébé. Thus, this couple sitting on the *imago mundi* probably testifies to the Peul occupation, or more precisely to a population that sprang from the alliance between the warrior Peuls and another people, possibly blacksmiths. This alliance, in order to be made concrete and maintained, was probably legitimized by registering, for the benefit of the conquered people, its eloquent and authoritarian image in the mythic structure of the Dogon country. We might add that the style of the caryatid figures is identical with that of the forty-four figures in relief on the granary shutter (no. 74) which can be assumed to be an index of the forty-four peoples descended from Mande. Wood. Height 29 in. (74 cm.)

38. Primordial Couple seated on columns. The man's left arm is around the woman's shoulders. The woman wears numerous bracelets on each arm. Both have horseshoe-shaped ears, like those of *nommos*. All the same, the general style, and especially that of the heads, is very similar to the style of the Bambara. Thus, this couple too, like no. 37, may bear witness to a foreign occupation yielding to the mythic structure of the conquered people. Wood. Height 22½ in. (57.2 cm.)

39. *Hogon* seated on an *imago mundi* stool. The *hogon* can be identified by his beard and the headgear indicated by incised lines on the skull. The four caryatid figures have been simplified to four bent forms. The lower disk has been cut out. There is no *axis mundi*. Wood. Height 21 in. (53.5 cm.)

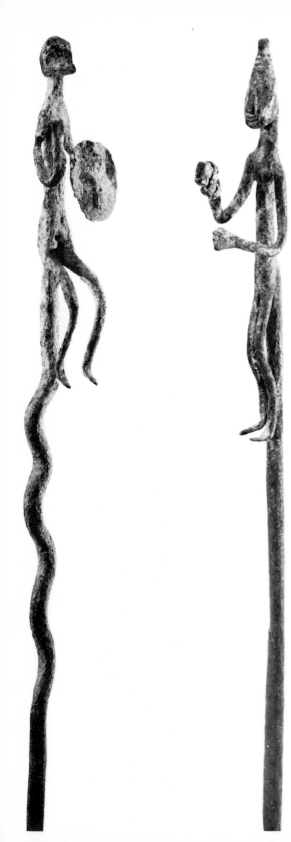

After the sacrifice of the fifth *nommo* and the scattering of his dismembered body over the earth, the seventh descended from the heavens. This was the blacksmith, who brought to earth the ancestors of human beings as well as animals, grain, and technology. Three versions of the myth differ in regard to the nature of the cosmic vehicle; it is described as an edifice in the shape of a truncated cone representing a granary filled with pure earth, as a sort of two-story vessel, or as an ark or ferry with the head of a horse or an antelope. The first version is found in similar form among the Fali of northern Cameroon. In the last version, the horse and rider are identified with the ark; the horse was the first animal to leave it.

The blacksmith robbed the heavenly workshops of a piece of the sun in the form of live coals and incandescent iron and then dashed down the rainbow with his prize, his descent proceeding along a spiral path. Irritated by the theft, those *nommos* who had remained in the sky attacked the thief. Twice they hurled a firebrand at him, and twice the blacksmith warded it off with the skin of his bellows, thus creating a shield that acquired the solar essence, having received a bit of the sun, so that fire could no longer prevail against it. So brutal was the impact of the blacksmith's landing on earth that the mace he carried in his arms and the anvil slung over his back smashed his sinuous limbs. Thus were created the joints—knees and elbows—which allow men to work and dance.

40. Helmsman-blacksmith, holding a shield in his left hand, on a wavy staff. The shield protects him from the attack of the other *nommos*. The wavy line of the staff refers to the spiral path of his fall. Iron. Height 48 in. (122 cm.)

41. Blacksmith with arms bent forward, legs bent and distinct, on a staff. Iron. Height 16 in. (40.5 cm.). Height of figure 6 in. (15.2 cm.)

42. Blacksmith carrying the crooked stick of the ritual thief on his right shoulder and a sheathed knife on his left arm. The beard and the four lines of herringbone pattern on the chest probably indicate that the blacksmith, like the *hogon*, partakes of the essence of the serpent Lébé. The apron around his loins is incised with signs that refer to the firebrands hurled at him by the other *nommos*. There is also a triangle composed of seven rows of herringbone pattern. Wood. Height 25 in. (63.5 cm.). Publ. Laude, 1964, slides 16–18

43. Helmsman-blacksmith (?) kneeling on a quadruped. Tellem style. The figure has horse-shoe-shaped ears and distinct breasts. Wood with heavy sacrificial patina. Height 17 in. (43.2 cm.). Publ. Meauzé, 1967, p. 154, fig. 2

44. Helmsman-blacksmith (?) kneeling on a quadruped. Tellem style. Wood. Height 11 in. (28 cm.). Length 17 in. (43.2 cm.)

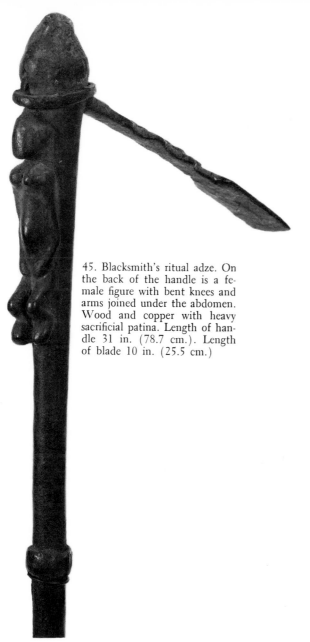

45. Blacksmith's ritual adze. On the back of the handle is a female figure with bent knees and arms joined under the abdomen. Wood and copper with heavy sacrificial patina. Length of handle 31 in. (78.7 cm.). Length of blade 10 in. (25.5 cm.)

46. Horse and rider. The horse is saddled and bridled. The whole piece, carved from a single block of wood, originally rested on a base, most of which is now missing along with the right front leg of the horse. This is probably a representation of a *hogon*, to judge by the beard and headdress. The breasts are distinct. The features are similar to those of a *hogon* seated on an *imago mundi* stool in the Klejman Collection. Wood. Height 21½ in. (54.6 cm.)

47. Horse and rider. The horse is saddled and bridled The rider grasps the reins in his left hand. The right arm is bent forward; the hand probably held a lance. On the upper left arm is a bracelet with herringbone pattern in relief. The hair is arranged in a double braid. The back is scarified with a herringbone line across the shoulders and along the vertebral column a motif that is analogous to but differs from the motif seen on the torsos of the Primordial Couple in the Barnes Foundation. The horse wears a collar similar to that in no. 46. Wood. Height 32 in. (81.3 cm.). Publ. Kunsthaus Zurich, 1970, p. 21, no. A3; Villa Hügel, 1971, p. 25, no. A3.

48. Ark in the form of a horse. The piece is hollow. On the lid are two representations in relief of Dyougou Serou hiding his face. The rounded flanks of the animal, as well as the legs, are decorated with geometrical motifs that refer to the primal field. Wood. Height 13½ in. (34 cm.). Length 22 in. (50.6 cm.)

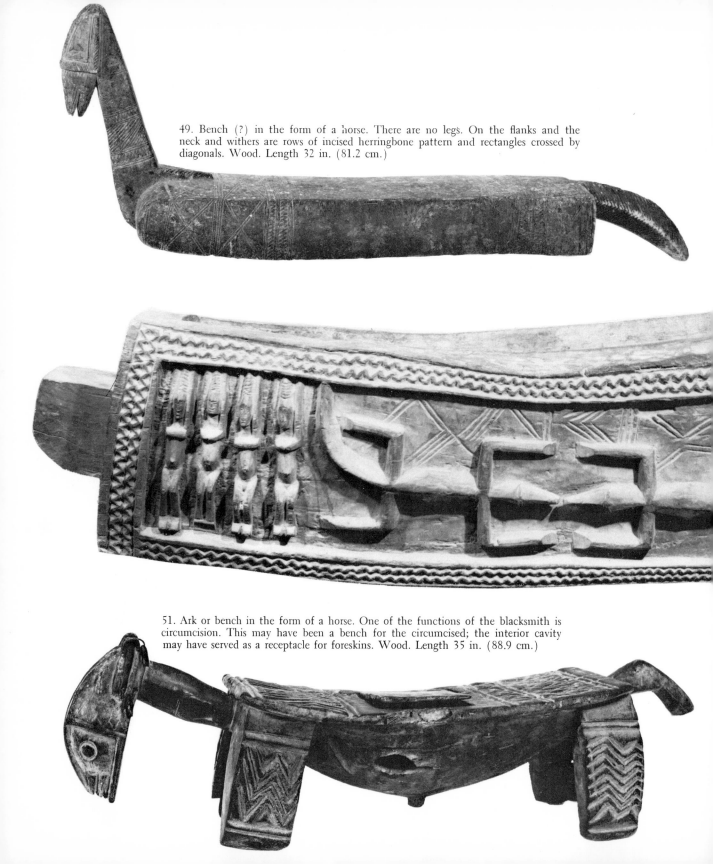

49. Bench (?) in the form of a horse. There are no legs. On the flanks and the neck and withers are rows of incised herringbone pattern and rectangles crossed by diagonals. Wood. Length 32 in. (81.2 cm.)

51. Ark or bench in the form of a horse. One of the functions of the blacksmith is circumcision. This may have been a bench for the circumcised; the interior cavity may have served as a receptacle for foreskins. Wood. Length 35 in. (88.9 cm.)

50. Ark with the head of a horse. On each side of this hollow ark are four pairs of *nommos* with raised arms and crocodiles, their tails erect, in sunk relief. The composition is framed by a double line of herringbone pattern. The horse wears a collar from which hang small iron bells. Wood. Length 65 in. (165 cm.). Publ. Laude, 1964, slides 27, 28

This work belongs to a group of three related objects, which includes the horse and rider in no. 47 and a third piece, a stake topped by two hemispheres joined by four bent forms, stylized *nommos* with raised arms. These three pieces seem to have some relation to warrior rites. The ark is said to have been used at the start of military operations for the performance of propitiatory rites and contained lustral water meant to purify the combatants. The theme of the horse is associated, among neighboring peoples (especially the Mossi), with war and a military aristocracy.

52. Female figure. Several figures identical in detail to this one are known. One, acquired in Ogol, is in the Musée de l'Homme; a second is in the Pierre Guerre Collection, Marseilles; and a third is in the Rietberg Museum, Zurich. They may be attributed with reasonable certainty to the same sculptor, who might be called the Master of Ogol. The Dogon call these figures *dege dal nda*, "statuettes on the terrace." Kept in the dwelling of the *hogon*, they were dressed and placed on the terrace of a dead person's house during his funeral. They were a privilege of rich families. They differ from one another only in the number of bracelets on the arms and of iron rings attached to the ears. They probably represent the master-blacksmith, here depicted with the female aspect dominant. The headdress, shaped like a crest, recalls that of the Peuls. The cylindrical motif under the chin is probably a displacement of the labret. Wood. Height 25 in. (63.5 cm.)

DONKEYS BEARING CUPS

During the celebration of the harvest, mutton and donkey meat are mixed in a cup and each person, beginning with the *hogon*, takes a piece and eats it. The *hogon* is identified with the millet seed that grows and dies in order to be reborn. At one time he was probably identified with the donkey, regarded by the Dogon as the animal closest to man because of its stubborn and independent nature; its name, in the Dogon language, is "*hogon* of Arou," probably the supreme *hogon*. It seems likely that at one time the *hogon* was ritually sacrificed and his flesh mixed in the cup along with that of animals. Thus, as Denise Paulme has pointed out, he can be added to the long list of divine kings in Black Africa. Eventually, the donkey with which he was identified was substituted for him. The geometrical motifs incised on the cups carried by donkeys recall the design of the primal field, the *hogon* field, which was purified by the sacrifice of a *nommo*. The identification of the *hogon* with the millet seed is made explicit by certain cups borne by donkeys with figures of women grinding millet on their lids.

According to Griaule (who identifies the animal as a horse), certain of the double cups were formerly brought out only for the "enthronement of a chief."

53. Double hemispherical cup supported by a donkey. On the lid is a second donkey, smaller and bridled, mounted by a *hogon* with arms bent at the elbows. The cup and lid are incised with patterns that include triangles and oblique parallel lines, which refer to the primal field. Wood. Height 33 in. (83.8 cm.)

DOGS

When the migrating Dogon arrived at the edge of the Bandiagara Cliff, they came into conflict with the Tellem, who jealously concealed the location of wells and water holes. Exhausted by their journey and parched by the drought, the Dogon saw one of their dogs come running with wet paws. They occupied the watering place discovered by the animal and, thus refreshed, were able to dislodge the Tellem from the Cliff. Depictions of dogs commemorate this important event in Dogon history. Some examples, including the one in the Museum of Primitive Art, have two figures wearing *hogon* headgear in relief on the flanks of the animal; these figures allude to the four *nommo* couples and to the four heads of lineage who led the migration: Arou, Ono, Dyon, and Domno. According to Desplagnes, who made his observations in 1907, there was a dog clan in the Dogon country, and the animal was ritually sacrificed, in all likelihood over his sculptured image. In some examples, the dog's tongue hangs out, and the tail may be decorated with a broken line, the symbol of water.

54. Dog. Wood with sacrificial patina. Height 9 in. (23 cm.). Length 15½ in. (39.5 cm.)

55. Standing woman carrying a child on her left arm. Her hands are crossed over the loincloth. She wears a necklace of small rectangular pieces, four bracelets around the wrist, and three more around the upper arm. The stylized chin should not be mistaken for a beard. Wood. Height 31 in. (78.7 cm.)

56. Kneeling woman with two children on her back and a third on her left arm. Wood, eroded, with sacrificial patina. Height 12½ in. (32 cm.)

WOMEN WITH CHILDREN

It is not known in what way these sculptures refer to mythic events. They are probably connected with the commemorative funerary rites (*dama* rites) that speed the departure of the dead person's soul from the world of the living.

57. Kneeling woman with a child on her back and another on each arm. Wood, eroded, with sacrificial patina. Height 13 in. (33 cm.)

58. Kneeling woman carrying a child on her back. Wood, damaged, with sacrificial patina. Height 9¾ in. (24.8 cm.)

UNIDENTIFIED OBJECTS

59. Male figure, standing, arms at his sides, hands joined below the abdomen. He wears a necklace with a pendant (?) and a cap. The nose is shaped like an upside-down T· and decorated with ladder pattern. Wood. Height 28 in. (71.2 cm.)

60. Female figure, arms at her sides, and distinct legs, on a short staff terminating in a rounded finial decorated with eight ridges, probably a reference to the eight *nommos*. A round stone (probably a marriage stone or *duge*) is inserted into the body. Wood and stone. Height 18 in. (45.7 cm.)

61. Androgynous figure with distinct breasts and legs, male genital, arms at the sides. He wears a hemispherical skullcap. This type of sculpture was buried in the ground when a village was established. Wood with heavy sacrificial patina. Height 40 in. (101.5 cm.)

62. Female figure, breasts and legs distinct, arms bent (?) along the body. She wears a hemispherical skullcap. Wood, much eroded. Height 27½ in. (69.8 cm.)

63. Standing female figure, breasts and legs distinct, arms down the sides and hands folded over the abdomen. Wood. Height 25½ in. (54.7 cm.)

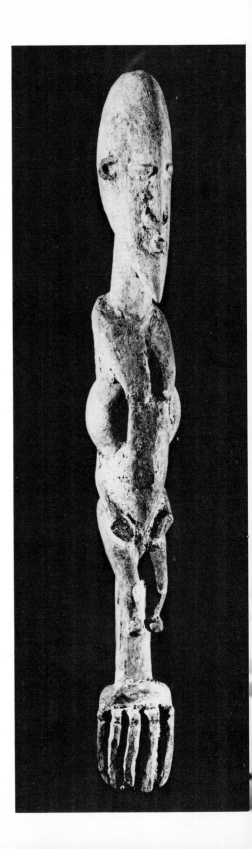

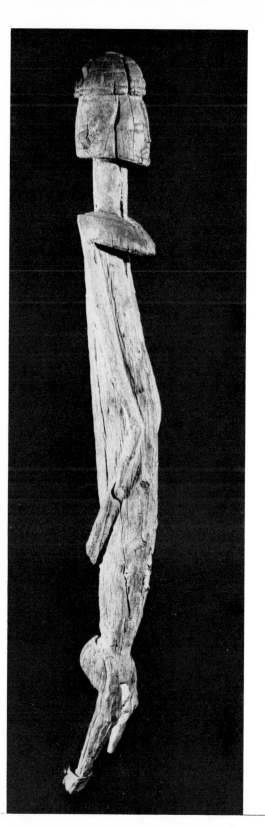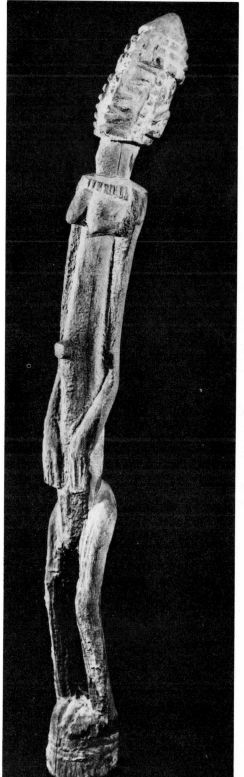

64. Wooden slab in the form of a stirrup surmounted by a hook (?) in the shape of a profile head. Three standing male figures are cut into the center of the slab and are seen in front view from both sides. All have distinct legs and arms at their sides, joined under the abdomen. All wear labrets, and the center figure has an iron bell around his neck. On one side a serpent in relief above the figures, on the other side a crocodile. Wood with sacrificial patina and iron. Height 19 in. (48.3 cm.)

65. Human head, scarified in relief with spiral motifs and a serpentine line on the forehead and parallel lines on the cheeks and sides of the face. This unique object may have been attached to a stave or shaft. To be attributed to the Dogon only with great reservations. Copper or brass, *cire perdue*. Height 7½ in. (19 cm.)

66. Bull with two strands of beads encircling the body. This piece allegedly comes from the region of Bankasse, an area rich in unusual objects. So far as we know, neither the bull nor the cow plays any role in Dogon myth, but they are important to the Peuls, who, in the region of Bankasse, are neighbors of the Dogon. The attribution of this piece cannot be determined with certainty. Wood and glass beads. Height 8 in. (20.3 cm.). Length 20 in. (50.8 cm.)

67. *Nommo* seated on a staff and holding in each hand a lance pointed at the sky. Iron. Height 59 in. (150 cm.). Height of figure 12 in. (30.5 cm.)

68. Head. Probably a fragment of a figurine. The mouth is open, revealing the teeth. Nostril holes are indicated. Terracotta, hollow. Height 6¾ in. (17.2 cm.)

69. Seated woman, hands folded under the chest. The face is incised with crosshatching. The legs are broken off. This piece, thought to have been collected by Griaule, is dated to about A.D. 1450. Terracotta, solid. Height 11 in. (28 cm.)

TOGUNA POSTS

In the northern part of a Dogon village, near the forge, is an open shed consisting of a roof supported by forked posts, which are carved on the outside. Here, in the *toguna*, the men meet to discuss village affairs or simply to rest. Women are not allowed inside. The posts of the *toguna*, along with granary doors and shutters, are the only sculptural manifestations of the Dogon that can be regarded as architectural. The decoration of *toguna* posts would seem to be limited to representations of women with highly developed breasts, couples, and birds, all linked to fertility beliefs. The pieces shown here probably came from the Plain of Seno, which is subject to influences of many kinds.

70. Primordial Couple. Sexual attributes are clearly specified. Under each foot is a footprint. The square face and treatment of the chest recall Bambara sculpture. Wood. Height 75 in. (190.5 cm.)

71. Standing woman with highly developed breasts. The exaggeration of the breasts recalls Bambara sculpture. Wood, base of post much eroded. Height 52 in. (132 cm.). Publ. Leiris and Delange, 1968, p. 188, fig. 208

72. Standing woman. This piece is probably cut from a *toguna* post. The torso is shown in front view, but legs and feet are in profile and the feet are seen from above. The abdomen is scarified. Iron bracelets and earrings. Wood. Height 27 in. (68.5 cm.)

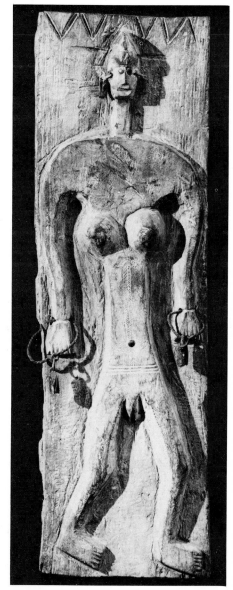

GRANARY SHUTTERS

The decoration of a granary shutter expresses the owner's relationship to the altar or *binu* of his people. The entire surface of the shutter is covered with figures in relief. The lock also bears a motif that identifies it specifically with the owner.

73. One-piece granary shutter decorated with a stylized crocodile. On the left, near the hinge pins, are two standing figures, one above the other, with arms at their sides. On each side of the animal's head is a standing figure, arms at his sides. On each side of the tail, Dyougou Serou hiding his face. Wood. Height 28 in. (71 cm.). Width 19 in. (48.2 cm.)

74. Granary shutter in two parts connected with four iron clasps and decorated with forty-four standing figures, arms at their sides, their legs distinct and bent. This composition is probably an allusion to the forty-four peoples descended from Mande. Wood and iron. Height 29 in. (73.6 cm.). Width 18½ in. (47 cm.)

SMALL OBJECTS IN COPPER OR BRASS

These objects were all cast by the *cire perdue* process. The rings may have been the insignia of dignitaries or merely tokens of gratitude.

75. Figurine, seated, hands on knees. Height 1¾ in. (4.5 cm.)

76. Ring with three concentric disks. Height 1¼ in. (3.2 cm.)

78. Ring with horse and rider. Height 3½ in. (9 cm.)

77. Ring in the form of a skullcap (?). Height 2 in. (5 cm.)

80. Ring with two chameleons. Height 1½ in. (4 cm.)

79. Ring with scorpion. Height 1½ in. (4 cm.)

81. Figurine, seated, legs drawn up to the belly. Height 1¾ in. (4.5 cm.)

ANIMALS IN FORGED IRON

These figures were placed on family altars and probably indicated the family's specific totem.

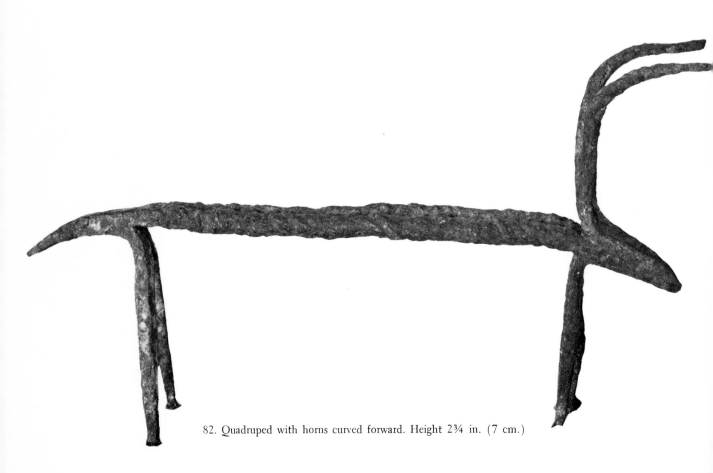

82. Quadruped with horns curved forward. Height 2¾ in. (7 cm.)

83. Dromedary. Height 3¾ in. (9.5 cm.)

STONE PAINTINGS

The Great Masks (no. 89) are gigantic structures of enormous ritual importance which are never worn. The rock shelters in which they are kept are decorated with painted figures, generally in red ochre, whose purpose is to contain the excess of vital force (*nyama*) trapped and controlled in the masks. If the *nyama* were allowed to roam at will, it would be dangerous to the people. These figures are periodically repainted, especially when young men are circumcised.

84. Lizard (*ugulu*). The stylized shape of the body is reminiscent of the structure of the *kanaga* mask (no. 98). Stone, painted. Height 10½ in. (26.7 cm.)

85. Pulley support for a loom. On the legs are two seated *nommos*, arms at their sides, joined by a bridge decorated with herringbone pattern, which here alludes particularly to the movement of the thread in the weft. Wood. Height 7½ in. (19 cm.)

86. Incised bowl. Wood. Height 5 in. (12.7 cm.). Diameter 9 in. (23 cm.)

87. Shoulder drum, decorated with figures in relief, arms at their sides, hands joined below the abdomen, and braincases removed. Wood, hide, liana fiber. Height 16 in. (40.5 cm.). Diameter 6¼ in. (16 cm.)

88. Incised bowl with handle. Wood. Height 4 in. (10 cm.). Diameter 8 in. (20.3 cm.)

MASKS

Masks are carved by those who will wear them in ritual performances. The mask proper is only part of a costume made of fibers that covers most of the body. It traps and controls vital force that would be dangerous if allowed to wander but can be redistributed for the benefit of society during performances of the *awa* or mask society. According to Griaule, the word *awa* is equivalent to the Greek word *cosmos*.

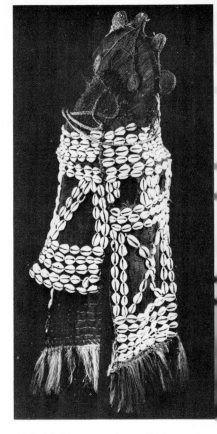

90. Mask representing a Peul woman. Cotton cloth, woven and braided raffia, and cowrie shells. Height 23½ in. (59.7 cm.)

89. Great Mask or "Mother of Masks." Great Masks were never worn. They were carved every sixty years for the *sigui* festival, and once it was over, they were stored with their predecessors. This one was acquired in 1931 by Griaule, who estimated that it went back to the first half of the eighteenth century. Wood, eroded, with traces of red and black paint. Height 109 in. (277 cm.)

91. Fragment of a Great Mask. Wood, eroded. Height 20½ in. (52 cm.)

92. *Samo* mask. Wood with traces of black paint. Height 16 in. (41 cm.). Publ. Leiris and Delange, 1968, p. 273, no. 306

93. Antelope mask. The wearer dances, holding a stick with which he pretends to dig in the ground in order to plant seeds. The *nyama* of this animal, the *walu* or "bush horse," is supposed to be particularly fearful. Wood with brown, black, and white paint. Height 19½ in. (49.5 cm.)

94. Black monkey mask. Allegedly acquired by Griaule in Ireli in 1931. Wood. Height 16 in. (40.5 cm.)

95. Buffalo mask. Wood with black and white paint.
Height 24 in. (61 cm.)

96. Antelope (*walu*) mask. Former Collection
Marcel Griaule (?). Wood with black and white
paint. Height 36 in. (91.5 cm.)

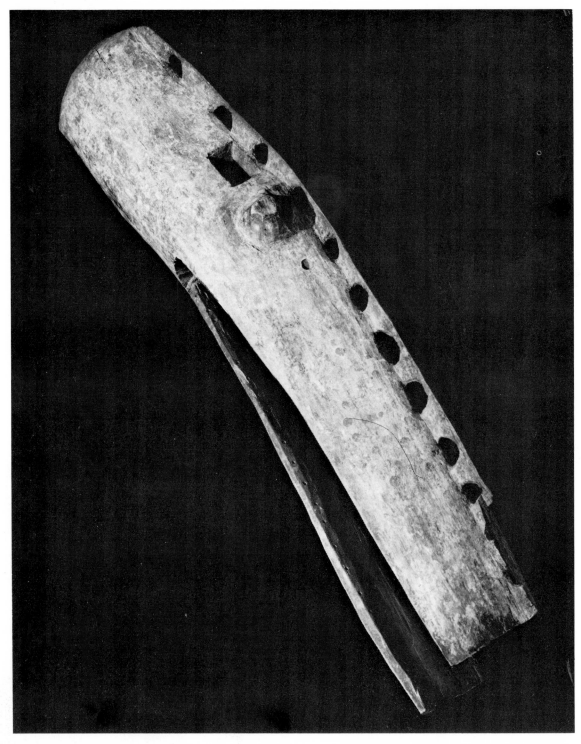

97. Crocodile mask, worn horizontally on top of the head. Wood with traces of black and red paint. Length 39 in. (99 cm.)

98. *Kanaga* mask. Wood with black and white paint and netted rope fiber. Height 36 in. (91.5 cm.). Width 23 in. (58.5 cm.)

99. White monkey mask. Former Collection Marcel Griaule (?). Wood with traces of sacrificial patina. Height 18 in. (45.7 cm.)

100. *Sim* mask. This rare mask, which resembles the *kanaga*, is composed of an antelope mask surmounted by a flexible superstructure of palm wood. Wood with traces of black, red, and white paint, rattan, and palm fiber. Height 65 in. (165 cm.)

101. Rhinoceros (*gomintogo*) mask. This mask is worn by a dancer who holds a stick with which he scrapes the soil. Wood with black and white paint. Height 29 in. (73.5 cm.)

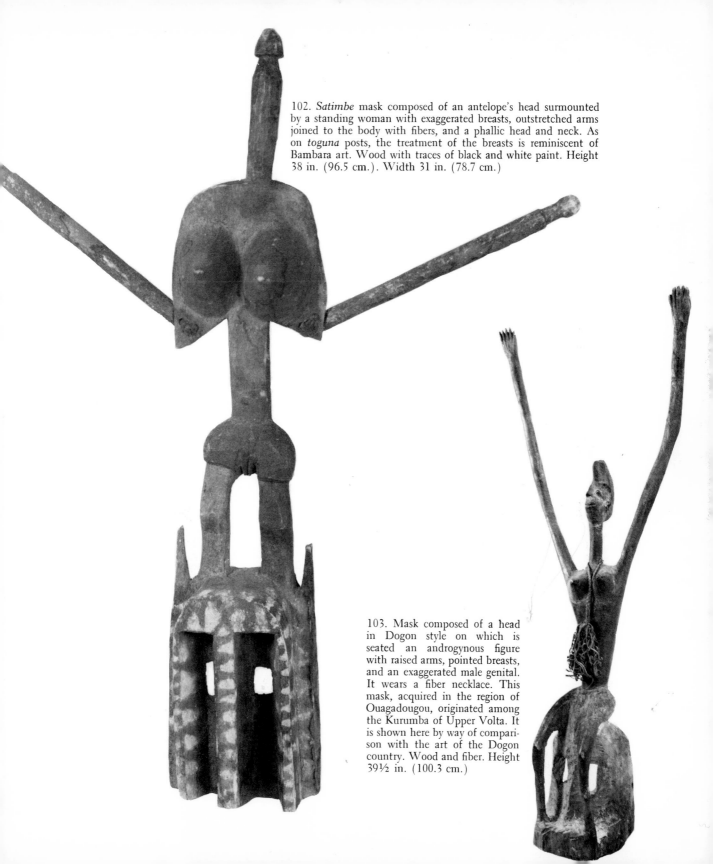

102. *Satimbe* mask composed of an antelope's head surmounted by a standing woman with exaggerated breasts, outstretched arms joined to the body with fibers, and a phallic head and neck. As on *toguna* posts, the treatment of the breasts is reminiscent of Bambara art. Wood with traces of black and white paint. Height 38 in. (96.5 cm.). Width 31 in. (78.7 cm.)

103. Mask composed of a head in Dogon style on which is seated an androgynous figure with raised arms, pointed breasts, and an exaggerated male genital. It wears a fiber necklace. This mask, acquired in the region of Ouagadougou, originated among the Kurumba of Upper Volta. It is shown here by way of comparison with the art of the Dogon country. Wood and fiber. Height 39½ in. (100.3 cm.)

BIBLIOGRAPHY OF WORKS CITED

Griaule, 1965 — Griaule, Marcel. *Conversations with Ogotemmêli: An Introduction to Dogon Religious Ideas.* London: Oxford University Press, 1965. Originally published as *Dieu d'eau: Entretiens avec Ogotemmêli.* Paris: Editions du Chêne, 1948.

Hanover Gallery, 1959 — London, Hanover Gallery. *Sculpture of the Tellem and the Dogon.* Text by Michel Leiris and Jacques Damase. London: Hanover Gallery, 1959.

Kjersmeier, 1935 — Kjersmeier, Carl. *Centres de style de la sculpture nègre africaine.* 4 vols. Paris: Morancé, 1935–38.

Kunsthaus Zürich, 1970 — Zürich, Kunsthaus Zürich. *Die Kunst von Schwarz-Afrika.* Text by Elsy Leuzinger. Recklinghausen: Verlag Aurel Bongers, 1970.

Langlois, 1954 — Langlois, Pierre. *Arts soudanais: Tribus Dogons.* Brussels: Editions de la Connaissance; Lille: Librarie Marcel Evrard, 1954.

Laude, 1964 — Laude, Jean. "La statuaire du pays Dogon." *Revue d'esthétique* 17 (1964), pp. 46–68.

Laude, 1964 (slides) — Laude, Jean. *Arts d'Afrique noire.* Paris: Ministère de la Coopération, 1964. Collection of 100 slides with descriptive brochure.

Laude, 1968 (slides) — Laude, Jean. *Les arts de l'Afrique noire.* Paris: Institut Pédagogique National, 1968. Collection of 100 slides with descriptive brochure.

Laude, 1971 — Laude, Jean. *The Arts of Black Africa.* Translated by Jean Decock. Berkeley and Los Angeles: University of California Press, 1971. Originally published as *Les arts de l'Afrique noire.* Paris: Librairie Générale Française, 1966.

Leiris and Delange, 1968 — Leiris, Michel, and Delange, Jacqueline. *African Art.* Translated by Michael Ross. New York: Golden Press, 1968. Originally published as *Afrique noire: La création artistique.* Paris: Gallimard, 1967.

Lem, 1948 — Lem, F.-H. *Sculptures soudanaises.* Paris: Arts et Métiers Graphiques, 1948.

Leuzinger, 1967 — Leuzinger, Elsy. *Africa: The Art of the Negro Peoples.* Translated by Ann E. Keep. 2nd ed. New York: Crown Publishers, 1967. French edition: *Afrique: Art des peuples noirs.* Paris: A. Michel, 1962.

Meauzé, 1967 — Meauzé, P. *L'Art nègre.* Paris: Hachette, 1967.

Museum of Primitive Art, 1959 — New York, The Museum of Primitive Art. *Sculpture from Three African Tribes: Senufo, Baga, Dogon.* Introduction by Robert Goldwater. New York: Museum of Primitive Art, 1959.

Palais Granvelle, 1958 — Besançon, Palais Granvelle. *L'Art de l'Afrique noire.* Text by Jacqueline Delange. Besançon: Palais Granvelle, 1958.

University Museum, 1956 — Philadelphia, The University Museum. *African Tribal Sculpture.* Text by Margaret Plass. Philadelphia: University Museum, 1956.

Villa Hügel, 1971 — Essen, Villa Hügel. *Afrikanische Kunstwerke: Kulturen am Niger.* Text by Elsy Leuzinger. Recklinghausen: Verlag Aurel Bongers, 1971.

ADDITIONAL BIBLIOGRAPHY

General Works

Griaule, Marcel. *Folk Art of Black Africa*. Translated by Michael Heron. New York: Tudor, 1950. Originally published as *Arts de l'Afrique noire*. Paris: Éditions du Chêne, 1947.

Minotaure, no. 2 (June 1933). Special issue devoted entirely to the Mission Dakar-Djibouti, 1931–33. Articles by P. Rivet, G. H. Rivière, M. Griaule, M. Leiris, A. Schaeffner et al.

Dogon Arts and Architecture

Calame-Griaule, Geneviève. "Notes sur l'habitation du plateau central nigérien (région de Bandiagara)." *Bulletin de l'Institut français d'Afrique noire* (Dakar), ser. B, 17 (1955), pp. 477–99.

Flam, Jack D. "Some Aspects of Style Symbolism in Sudanese Sculpture." *Journal de la Société des africanistes* 40 (1970), pp. 137–50.

Griaule, Marcel. *Masques dogons*. Travaux et mémoires de l'Institut d'ethnologie, Université de Paris, no. 33. Paris: Institut d'ethnologie, 1938.

Imperato, Pascal J. "Contemporary Adapted Dances of the Dogon." *African Arts* 5 (1971), p. 28.

Laude, Jean. "Esthétique et système de classification: La statuaire africaine." *Sciences de l'art*, no. 2 (1965), pp. 57–85.

New York, Galerie Kamer. *Iron Sculpture of the Dogon*. Text by Jean Laude. New York: Galerie Kamer, 1964.

Dogon Religion and Symbolism

Calame-Griaule, Geneviève. *Ethnologie et langage: La parole chez les dogon*. Paris: Gallimard, 1965.

Dieterlen, Germaine. *Les âmes des Dogons*. Travaux et mémoires de l'Institut d'ethnologie, Université de Paris, no. 40. Paris: Institut d'ethnologie, 1941.

Griaule, Marcel. "Art et symbole en Afrique noire." *Zodiaque: Cahiers de l'Atelier du Coeur meurtri* 2, no. 5 (October 1951), p. 35.

Griaule, Marcel. "Les symboles des arts africains." *Présence africaine*, nos. 10–11 (1951), pp. 12–24.

Griaule, Marcel, and Dieterlen, Germaine. "The Dogon." In *African Worlds*, edited by Daryll Forde. London: Oxford University Press, 1954.

Griaule, Marcel, and Dieterlen, Germaine. *Le renard pâle*. Travaux et mémoires de l'Institut d'ethnologie, Université de Paris, no. 72. Paris: Institut d'ethnologie, 1965.

Leiris, Michel. *La langue secrète des Dogons de Sanga (Soudan français)*. Travaux et mémoires de l'Institut d'ethnologie, Université de Paris, no. 50. Paris: Institut d'ethnologie, 1948.

Zahan, Dominique. "Aperçu sur la pensée théogonique des Dogon." *Cahiers internationaux de sociologie* 6 (1949), pp. 113–33.

Dogon Social Organization

Arnaud, Robert. "Notes sur les montagnards Habé des cercles de Bandiagara et de Hombori (Soudan français)." *Revue d'ethnographie et des traditions populaires* 2 (1921), pp. 241–314.

Desplagnes, Lieutenant Louis. *Le plateau central nigérien: Une mission archéologique et ethnographique au Soudan français*. Paris: Larose, 1907.

Ganay, Solange de. *Les devises des Dogons*. Travaux et mémoires de l'Institut d'ethnologie, Université de Paris, no. 41. Paris: Institut d'ethnologie, 1941.

Marti, Monserrat P. *Les Dogon*. Paris: Presses Universitaires de France, 1957.

Paulme, Denise. *Organization sociale des Dogon (Soudan français)*. Etudes de sociologie et d'ethnologie juridiques, Institut de droit comparé, no. 32. Paris: Domat-Montchrestien, 1940.